SMALL ARMS
PISTOLS AND RIFLES

GREENHILL MILITARY MANUALS

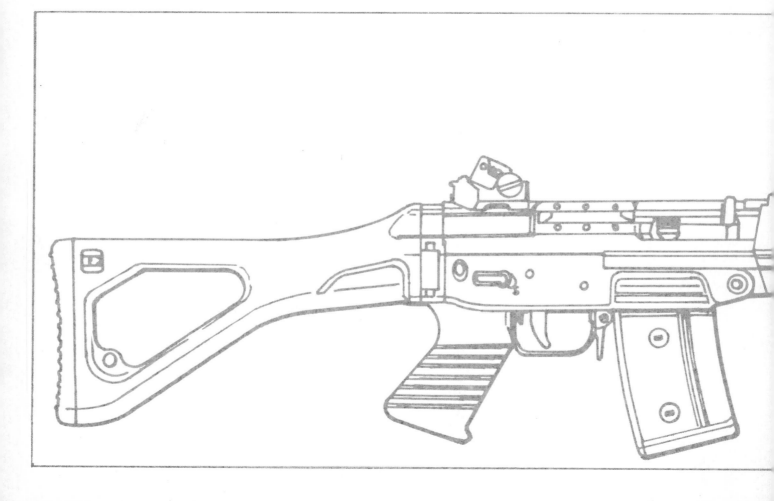

SMALL ARMS
PISTOLS & RIFLES

IAN V. HOGG

ILLUSTRATED BY RAY HUTCHINS

GREENHILL MILITARY MANUALS

Greenhill Books, London

Stackpole Books, Pennsylvania

Small Arms, Pistols & Rifles
first published 1994 by
Greenhill Books, Lionel Leventhal Limited, Park House,
1 Russell Gardens, London NW11 9NN
and
Stackpole Books, 5067 Ritter Road, Mechanicsburg, PA 117055, USA

British Library Cataloguing in Publication Data
Hogg, Ian V.
Small Arms, Pistols & Rifles – (Greenhill Military Manuals)
I. Title   II. Series   623.4
ISBN 1-85367-175-4

Library of Congress Cataloging-in-Publication Data
Hogg, Ian V.
Small Arms, Pistols & Rifles/by Alan K. Russell.
p. cm. – (Greenhill military manuals)
ISBN 1-85367-175-4 (hc) : $19.95
1. Tanks (Military science) – Handbook, manuals, etc.
2. Vehicles, Military – Handbooks, manuals, etc.
I. Title.   II. Series.
UG446.5.R73 1994   93-36814
358.1'883-dc20   CIP

Typeset by Merlin Publications
Printed and bound in Great Britain by
Butler & Tanner Ltd, Frome and London

Introduction

1993 sees the centenary of the first automatic pistol to be manufactured for commercial sale; this was the celebrated Borchardt, which went on to father the better-known Parabellum or Luger pistol and which served as an inspiration to many inventors.

The same year also witnessed a handful of automatic rifles, though entirely in the hands of their inventors, for no army was rash enough to stake its existence on such an untried weapon. It was to be another forty years or so before any major army took the plunge and made an automatic rifle its standard infantry arm.

The past 100 years has seen a constant procession of innovative ideas and new designs. It would be rash to say that firearms have reached the zenith of their development; but I think it true to say that they have now reached a level of technical excellence from which it will be extremely difficult to move on, and prohibitively expensive, in relation to any advantages gained, to attempt to do so. In recent years the United States Army has expended several hundreds of millions of dollars in a competition to find an Advanced Combat Rifle. After several years of work, four competing designs were exhaustively tested, and the results, carefully analysed, showed that the degree of improvement over the current service rifle was simply not worth the cost of replacement.

Similarly, it is probable that innovation is becoming rare because the expense is beyond the pocket of private companies. The days when a lone inventor laboured over his brain-child in a humble workshop, then took it to a manufacturing company to be turned into a profitable venture are almost over. Today it requires vast expenditure in research and development to bring a weapon to the point of production, and few companies any longer have such financial resources. The future of firearms development lies in international co-operation or state subsidies; or both.

All of which is by way of a preamble to introducing you to the remainder of this book, which is a representative showcase of modern, and some not so modern, rifles and pistols. Here are one or two elderly designs, to remind us of what went before, and a greater number of modern designs to indicate the way in which firearms design has progressed in the second half of the twentieth century. Certain features recur; some mechanical ideas have been so widely accepted that almost every current designer applies them without stopping to think whether the solution might be reached by another means; one has only to see the number of modern automatic pistols locking the breech into the ejection opening, or the number of gas-operated rifles using rotating bolts in a carrier, to see this commonality. Yet if you examine the patent records of the late 19th century you will find most of today's mechanisms and ideas laid out before you; the reason that it has taken so long to put them into practice is simply that the technology of the 19th century was some way behind the ingenuity of the inventors.

Nevertheless, what we have laid out for your inspection in the following pages can be considered as the state of the firearms art as it stands in the final decade of the twentieth century. And with the current move towards the reduction of forces and the clamour for the 'peace dividend' it seems probable that the art will remain at this level until well into the twenty-first century.

The Future

1. Some designs will go on forever. This is the Browning BDA9 double-action automatic pistol, and as the component parts show, the mechanism is very little different to the first Colt automatic pistol developed by John Moses Browning in 1900. Browning improved his design after the First World War, and after being delayed by the economic slump in the early 1930s, it appeared as the Browning High-Power in 1935. This lasted unchanged for over fifty years, after which a double-action trigger mechanism changed it into the BDA9. There is no reason why this pistol should not make another fifty years of service; why change something when it is perfectly good?

2. Some designs defy all the odds and survive long past their sell-by date. This Afghan guerrilla is examining a Soviet Stechkin full-automatic pistol taken from a downed Soviet pilot. The Stechkin was virtually a mini-submachine gun, and almost uncontrollable. It did not last long in Soviet service, but was later disposed of to various places and will doubtless appear for several years yet in sundry trouble spots.

4. The rifle firing caseless ammunition has been tempting designers since the 1940s. The principal advantage is the saving in brass and hence weight – the man can carry three times as much ammunition as for a conventional rifle. The technical problems were immense, but were successfully solved in the late 1970s. The next ten years were taken up with perfecting the principles into a design which could be economically manufactured. This done, the design was ready for adoption when the entire world strategic picture changed overnight, the threat of Soviet aggression appeared to vanish, and governments dramatically cut the amount of money they were prepared to spend on defence. The first victim was the caseless-cartridge rifle. It may re-appear in the next century; or not, as the case may be.

3. The assault rifle has become the universal infantry arm, superseding the full-sized rifle firing a long-range cartridge. In conjunction, as here, with a sight capable of seeing in starlight, it becomes a formidable weapon which gives the soldier command of the battlefield throughout the entire 24 hours. The only problem technology has yet to solve is how to keep him awake for 24 hours every day.

Contents

GLOCK MODEL 17 Austria

Manufacturer: Glock Ges.mbH, Deutsche Wagram
(Variant Models: Models 17L, 18, 19, 20, 21, 22 and 23)

In the early 1980s the Austrian Army selected the **Glock 17** as their new service pistol. The Glock company were known for their manufacture of bayonets, knives and edged tools, but they had never ventured into the firearms business before, and their appearance with this novel and practical weapon was something of a shock. After the Austrian Army, the pistol was adopted by India, Jordan, Norway, The Philippines, Thailand and several other military and police forces around the world.

The **Glock 17** is a recoil-operated pistol, using the familiar Browning system of dropping barrel controlled by a cam surface, and using the squared-off area of the breech to lock directly into the ejection port. No hammer is used; instead there is a self-cocking striker system. The first 5mm of trigger movement cocks the striker and releases an automatic firing pin safety lock. Further pressure on the trigger then releases the striker to fire the cartridge. There is no manual safety catch, but there is a small safety spur on the trigger.

Much of the **Glock** pistol is made from synthetic material, with the metal components moulded in; this gave rise to scare stories in the popular press, suggesting that the weapon would be a gift to terrorists since it would be invisible to airport X-Ray search. In fact some 60% of the weapon is of steel, and any X-Ray device will detect it instantly.

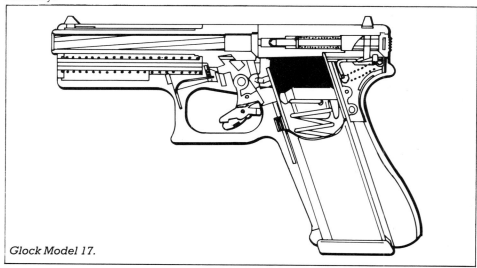

Glock Model 17.

The **Model 17L** is a long-barrelled model for target shooting; the **Model 19** is a 'compact' model, slightly shorter (177mm as against 188mm) than the **Model 17**.

The **Glock 18** was developed from the **Model 17** by the addition of a fire selector mechanism and enlarging the magazine capacity, turning the weapon into a machine pistol capable of automatic fire. In order to prevent unauthorised conversions, the main components of the **Models 17** and **18** are not interchangeable. The basic mechanism remains the same, but the result is a somewhat larger pistol.

In order to cater for those requiring heavier calibres, the **Models 20** and **21** were introduced in 1991. These are generally the same as the standard **Glock 17** but in heavier calibres; the **Model 20** in 10mm Auto, the **Model 21** in ·45 ACP. As might be expected they are slightly longer and heavier than the **Model 17**. Shortly after that the **Models 22** and **23** appeared. The **Model 22** is generally the same as the **Model 17** but in ·40 Smith & Wesson calibre, while the **Model 23** is the ·40 version of the **Model 19**, i.e., the compact ·40 design.

Specification (for Model 17):
Calibre: 9mm Parabellum
Operation: Short recoil, semi-automatic
Length overall: 188mm
Weight, empty: 650g
Barrel: 114mm, 6 grooves, right-hand twist
Magazine: 17-round box
Muzzle velocity: 350 m/sec

Glock Model 17L with 153mm barrel.

The 10mm calibre Model 20.

Machine pistol Model 18 with the optional 33-round extended magazine.

BROWNING GP-35 (High Power)   Belgium

Manufacturer: FN Herstal SA, Herstal
(Variant Models: Mark 2, Mark 3, Mark 3S)

This is one of the oldest military pistols in regular service, having been designed in the 1920s. Design actually began before 1914, as John Browning set about improving his Colt M1911 design. His principal changes were to the trigger linkage and the method of unlocking the barrel from the slide; in place of his original hinged link, he devised a solid block of metal with a curved slotted path which engaged with the slide stop pin to unlock the barrel. Due to World War One it was not until the early 1920s that Browning went to FN of Liége with his ideas. He died in 1926 and the work was continued by Dieudonné Saive, FN's Chief Designer, who made another fundamental change, altering the pistol to 9mm calibre and developing a magazine holding 13 shots. He also changed Browning's original internal striker to an external hammer.

Due to the Depression the new design was shelved until put into production in 1935. It was immediately adopted by Belgium, Lithuania, Latvia and China, but only about 35,000 had been made by 1940 when the German occupation took over the factory. The pistol was continued in production for the German Army as the 'Pistole 640(b)'. The drawings were smuggled to Britain and then sent to Canada where the pistol was made both for the Canadian and British forces and for the Chinese Nationalist Army. The FN factory resumed production after the war and the **GP-35** was adopted by the British Army in 1954. In all, about 65 countries have officially adopted the **Browning GP-35**, most of whom still use it.

A **Mark 2** model appeared in the 1970s; this was the same pistol but with 'anatomical' grips, an ambidextrous safety catch, wider sights and an oxidised finish. Production of this model ceased in the early 1980s. In 1988 the **Mark 3** was introduced, which is practically the same but with more metal in the slide, various slight changes in interior dimensions to improve reliability, and sights which can be removed and exchanged for target sights if desired. A **Mark 3S** is made for police use; this has an automatic firing pin safety system added.

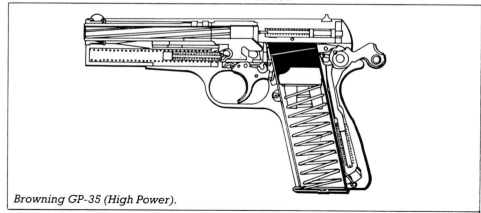

Browning GP-35 (High Power).

Specification:
Calibre: 9mm Parabellum
Operation: Short recoil, semi-automatic
Length overall: 197mm
Weight, empty: 990g
Barrel: 118mm, 6 grooves, right-hand twist, one turn in 250mm
Magazine: 13-round box
Muzzle velocity: 335 m/sec.

The Mk 3 version of the GP-35 shows differences in the safety catch, hammer, sights and grips but the mechanism beneath the skin is little changed since 1935.

The original High-Power of 1935 in its Canadian form, with a long-range sight and with the rear of the grip slotted to take a holster-stock, turning the pistol into a near-carbine. The drawing (far left) shows the shaped cam beneath the breech, Browning's replacement of his original swinging link.

FN DA 140   Belgium

Manufacturer: FN Herstall SA, Herstal
(Variant Model: BDA 380)

It is not generally known that FN Herstal SA and Pietro Beretta SpA owned portions of each other and worked together quite closely in several areas. FN have, since their earliest days, always been active in the production of 'pocket pistols' and small-calibre pistols for police use; indeed, the word 'Browning' is synonymous with 'small automatic pistol' in many European countries. But in the difficult markets of the 1980s it makes little sense to spend time devising something different just for the sake of being different when a measure of commercial cooperation can produce a satisfactory answer. And so when FN began contemplating a small police and self-defence pistol in the late 1970s it made sense for them to confer with Beretta and come up with an acceptable solution. The 9mm **FN 140 DA** (Double Action) pistol is, in effect, a slightly re-worked Beretta Model 81, so saving a great deal of design and development time.

The principal and visible difference is the use of an all-enveloping slide instead of the characteristic cut-away slide which is almost a trade-mark of Beretta designs. Apart from that, the double-action mechanism, large capacity magazine and duplication of the safety catch and slide stop lever on both sides are the same as the Beretta 81. The actual design of the safety catch and slide stop lever are slightly changed in their appearance, though not in their operation.

The **FN 140 DA** is available in either 7·65mm ACP or 9mm Short calibres. The BDA 380 is the American market model, sold under the Browning name in the USA, and is similarly available in both calibres. The 9mm Short version had found wide acceptance among police and security forces.

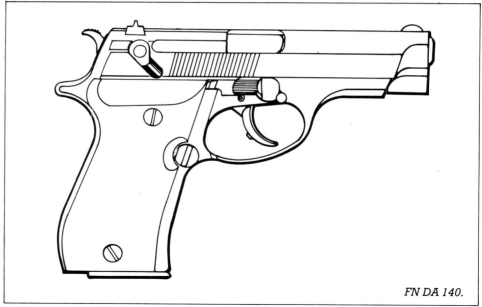

FN DA 140.

14

Specification:
Calibre: 9mm Short (·380 Auto)
Operation: Blowback, semi-automatic
Length: 173mm
Weight, empty: 640g
Barrel: 96mm, 6 grooves, right-hand twist
Magazine: 13-round box
Muzzle velocity: 290 m/sec.

The FN BDA 380 in 9mm Short (·380 Auto) calibre with the optional walnut grips.

The FN DA 140 in 7·65mm (·32 ACP) calibre is widely used by European police forces. Although modified by Fabrique Nationale to the Browning image, its Beretta origins can still be seen.

Manufacturer: FN Herstal SA, Herstal

In most respects the **BDA 9** is an enhanced **High-Power GP-35** model, using the same basic recoil action, method of breech locking and external hammer firing system. The principal change is the adoption of a double-action trigger mechanism of new design, allied to a de-cocking lever which is duplicated on both sides of the frame and an automatic firing pin safety system similar to that introduced in the Mark 3S GP-35. The magazine release catch is fitted for right-handed use but can be easily removed and also reversed so as to accommodate left-handed users.

The **BDA 9** is loaded in the usual manner by pulling back the slide and releasing it. This leaves the hammer cocked, and it can be fired by pulling the trigger. If it is not intended to fire, then the de-cocking lever is pressed up. This releases the hammer, which falls at moderate speed since it is slowed by a braking device and is stopped by the de-cocking safety notch before it can strike the firing pin. In any event, the firing pin is automatically locked in a safe condition, so that if the de-cocking safety failed, the hammer would still not fire the cartridge. With the hammer lowered in this manner the de-cocking lever is released and the pistol can now be carried safely. When required to fire, all that is necessary is to pull through on the trigger to raise the hammer to the full cock position and then release it. The final movement of the trigger which releases the hammer also raises the automatic safety block from engagement with the firing pin so that the falling hammer hits the pin, drives it forward and fires the cartridge.

The shape of the **BD** is unmistakably Browning, the only real difference between it and the GP-35 being the elongated trigger guard, necessary to permit the longer pull of a double-action trigger, which is also shaped at the front for a two-handed grip. The butt grips are shaped to give an anatomically correct gripping surface, and the rear sight is capable of lateral adjustment by an armourer.

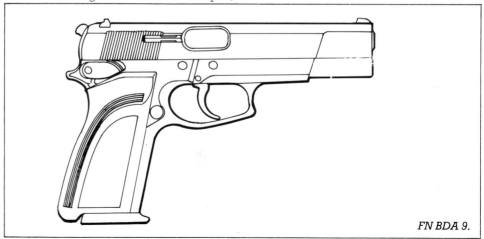

FN BDA 9.

Specification:
Calibre: 9mm Parabellum
Operation: Short recoil, semi-automatic
Length overall: 200mm
Weight, empty: 905g with empty magazine
Barrel: 118mm, 6 grooves, right-hand twist, one turn in 250mm
Magazine: 14-round box
Muzzle velocity: 350 m/sec.

The FN BDA9 is the double-action version of the older High-Power GP-35. The resemblance between this and the older pistol is easily seen, though there are small differences in the trigger-guard and an ambidextrous de-cocking lever has been added.

**Manufacturer: State arsenals
(Variant Model: Type 67)**

The **Type 64** is unusual in being built only with an integral silencer; there is no unsilenced version.

The frame is extended forward to carry the silencing system, which is a bulbous cylinder which contains a central wire mesh tube holding a number of rubber discs and which is surrounded by perforated metal sleeves. The fixed barrel is quite short, and after the bullet leaves the muzzle it passes into the wire mesh tube and through the series of rubber discs before leaving the end of the silencer. The gas which follows the bullet is forced to swirl around the perforated sleeves and is stopped from following the bullet by the self-sealing action of the rubber discs. This swirling gradually reduces the gas velocity and heat so that when the gas finally finds its way out at the front of the silencer it is moving comparatively slowly and generates almost no noise at all.

The rear of the frame carries a conventional type of slide which is driven back by the gas pressure in the fired case in the normal blowback manner. The slide contains a striker, which is cocked on the return stroke and held by a sear connected to the trigger. The slide is unusual in having a rotating-lug bolt head as its front end. There is a manual catch which can be set, after the breech has been closed, to lock the bolt to the barrel by means of the rotating head. Once this has been done, the blowback action is prevented and the breech remains closed after firing. The weapon is taken from the scene and at some location where noise is no longer important the slide is then unlocked and manually operated to eject the empty case and reload.

The cartridge used with this pistol is known as the 'Type 64' and is also unique; although it resembles the common ·32 ACP it is, in fact, rimless rather than semi-rimmed and the powder charge is specially selected to assist in the silencing.

The **Type 67** is an improved model; the principle of operation is the same but the silencer unit is a plain cylinder, making the weapon less bulky and easier to carry in a holster.

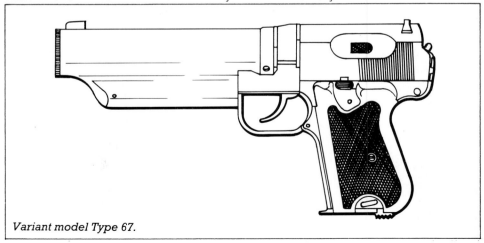

Variant model Type 67.

Specification:
Calibre: 7·65mm Type 64
Operation: Blowback, with locked breech option
Length overall: 222mm
Weight, empty: 1·81kg
Barrel: 95mm
Magazine: 9-round box
Muzzle velocity: 205 m/sec

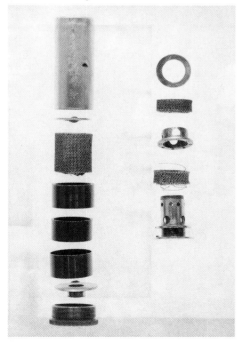

Left: the component parts of the Type 67 silencer, showing the gauze cylinders packed with absorbent material. The Type 64 layout is similar though of different shape.
Top: the Type 67 pistol is an improved Type 64, the silencer being a neater and more efficient design.
Right: the Type 67 pistol is an improved Type 64, this unique photograph shows a neater and more efficient design of silencer. It is purely for use by clandestine units, to remove sentries and guard dogs without alerting the neighbourhood.

Manufacturer: Česká Zbrojovka, Strakonice

The late 1940s demand of the Czech Army for a new pistol was complicated by the position of Czechoslovakia within the Soviet sphere of influence, which meant that any new pistol had to fire the Soviet 7·62mm cartridge, a powerful round demanding a locked breech. However, the Czechs, being individualists, decided to load the cartridge to a higher velocity than did the Soviets, and so the breech lock had to be substantial.

The result was a most unusual breech locking system, never used in any other pistol. In simple terms there is an overhang above the breech from which are suspended two rollers. When the breech is closed these rollers are forced out, by the shape of the overhang, into two recesses in the walls of the slide, and since the roller unit is attached to the barrel the slide and barrel are therefore locked together. On firing, everything recoils a short distance locked together, until the movement of a cam surface forces the rollers inwards and thus frees them from the slide. The barrel is then stopped, together with the roller

locking unit, and the slide is free to go back and extract and eject the spent case and cock the hammer. On the return movement it loads a fresh round and then forces the barrel unit forward until the cam surface drives the rollers back into the recesses and locks the breech once more.

This is a complex but very strong locking system, and one which was doubtless expensive to manufacture. It appears to be based on an idea first

patented by Mauser in 1910, later improved in Poland and finally perfected in the German MG42 machine gun, and to find such a system inside a pistol is quite remarkable.

The ČZ52 was only made for a few years and production stopped in about 1957. The guns remained in service for several years but since the early 1980s have been gradually replaced by the ČZ83, a simple blowback weapon.

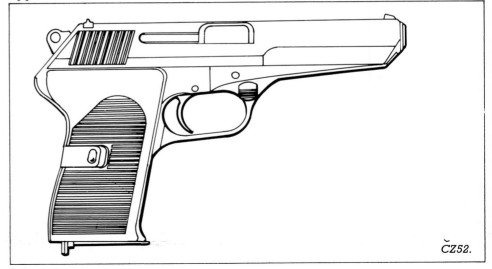

ČZ52.

Specification;
Calibre: 7·62mm Czech M48;
also 7·63mm Mauser
Operation: Short recoil, semi-automatic
Length overall: 209mm
Weight, empty: 960g
Barrel: 120mm, 4 grooves, right-hand twist
Magazine: 8-round box
Muzzle velocity: 457 m/sec

The CZ52 pistol field-stripped for cleaning.

Not all Warsaw Pact countries adhered to Soviet standard designs; the Czechs have a long tradition of firearms design and preferred their own pistol to that of their nominal masters. One reason for this was their adoption of a somewhat more powerful cartridge, demanding a more positive form of breech block.

21

ČZ75   Czechoslovakia

Manufacturer: Česká Zbrojovka, Uhersky Brod
(Variant Model: ČZ85)

This is not a Czech service pistol, because like all Warsaw Pact countries the Czechs do not use the 9mm Parabellum cartridge in military service. It was originally produced for export, and has been very successful in that respect, gaining a very high reputation for reliability and accuracy; it was later adopted by various elements of the Czech police force. The basic design has been copied by several other makers in various countries for commercial sale.

The ČZ75 is recoil-operated, using the well-tried Browning dropping barrel system, controlled by a shaped cam beneath the breech end. Slide and frame are precision castings carefully machined and well finished, and the grips are either of plastic or walnut. The trigger mechanism is double-action, and the slide-mounted safety catch disconnects the trigger from the hammer; it does not lower the hammer. It is of interest that the original design used a half-cock notch on the hammer; this was then removed at the insistence of production engineers to make manufacture simpler, but after two or three accidents reported from West Germany the half-cock notch was re-instated.

All the operating controls – safety catch, slide stop lever and magazine catch – are on the left side of the frame to suit right-handed firers. After several competing designs developed weapons with controls suited for right- or left-handed use, the ČZ85 pistol was developed. This is basically the same pistol but with the manual safety catch and slide stop lever duplicated on the right side of the weapon to make it convenient for left-handed use. The top of the slide is ribbed, to reduce light reflection, and some small internal changes have been made to simplify manufacture and also to improve the smooth action of the firing mechanism. The rear sight has been made laterally adjustable by means of a screw so that firers can make adjustments without requiring the services of a gunsmith. Both models are currently in production.

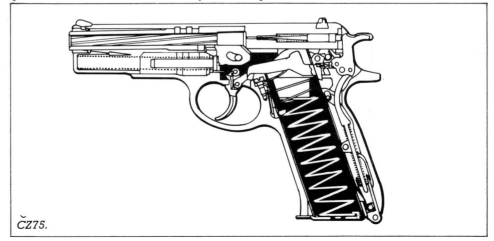

ČZ75.

Specification:
Calibre: 9mm Parabellum
Operation: Short recoil, semi-automatic
Length overall: 203mm
Weight, empty: 980g
Barrel: 120mm, 6 grooves, right-hand twist, one turn in 250mm
Magazine: 15-round box
Muzzle velocity: 338m/sec

Operating the safety catch on the ČZ85, an improved version of the original ČZ75.

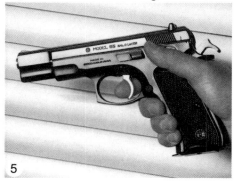

The ČZ75 was developed entirely for export, being a non-standard Warsaw Pact calibre. It has been widely sold abroad, and the simplicity of its construction has attracted a number of licensees and copyists in Britain, the USA, Italy and other countries.

MAB PA-15   France

Manufacturer: Manufacture d'Armes de Bayonne, Bayonne (Variant Models: PAPF-1)

In the 1970s the French Army required more pistols and instead of returning to St Etienne for more MAS50 weapons they turned to a commercial supplier, the Manufacture d'Armes de Bayonne. This firm had been producing pistols under the trade name 'Unique' for many years. Most of these were blowback pocket weapons in small calibres, but their 'Model R Para' was chambered for the 9mm Parabellum cartridge and adopted an unusual delayed blowback system of operation. The barrel and slide are locked together by a lug on top of the barrel, and another lug beneath the barrel engages in a curved track in the slide. On firing, the barrel and slide begin to move backwards locked together but at the same time the interaction of the lug and curved path rotates the barrel until the top locking lug is freed, after which the barrel stops and the slide continues moving backwards. The rotary movement of the barrel is resisted to some degree by torque due to the bullet engaging in the rifling, which attempts to turn the barrel in the opposite direction to that decreed by the unlocking lug and groove; the amount of delay is very minimal, but it is enough to let the bullet clear the muzzle before the breech opens.

The **PA-15**, as adopted by the Army, was the 'Model R Para' with the frame modified to accept a 15-shot magazine. It was a well-made weapon which was pleasant to shoot and which, due to the straight-line movement of the barrel, was inherently more accurate than a dropping-barrel design such as the MAS50. The French Army decided to take a further step for the benefit of their competition shooters and had a special model, the **PAPF-1**, made with the longer barrel and slide and an adjustable rear sight. There was also a **PA-8** model, which had an 8-shot magazine; this was actually the commercial 'Model R Para' with military acceptance marks.

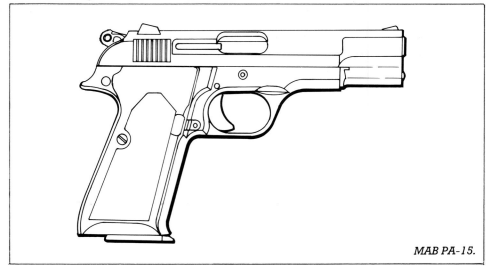

MAB PA-15.

24

Unfortunately the Manufacture d'Armes de Bayonne got into difficulties in the early 1980s and went into liquidation. This put the supply of pistols at hazard and with Army encouragement a new company was formed. This, though, also failed to prosper and when the armed forces next needed pistols they had to purchase the Beretta 92.

The PAPF-1 target model stripped for cleaning.

The PAPF-1 target model differs from the service PA-15 (drawing left) by having a longer barrel and a fully adjustable target pattern rear sight. The rotating barrel breech lock gives it an edge in accuracy and French military teams have put up a good performance in international contests.

Specification:
Calibre: 9mm Parabellum
Operation: Delayed blowback, semi-automatic
Length overall: 203mm
Weight, empty: 1070g
Barrel: 114mm, 6 grooves, right-hand twist
Magazine: 15-round box
Muzzle velocity: 335 m/sec.

HECKLER & KOCH P9S Germany

Manufacturer: Heckler & Koch GmbH, Oberndorf/Neckar (Variant Model: P9)

Heckler & Koch were founded in the late 1940s and after starting business by manufacturing machine tools produced a simple blowback pistol, the HK4. After this they developed the G3 rifle for the German Army. This involved the perfection of a roller-locked delayed blowback system of operation, and after seeing the rifle into production they applied the same breech system to a pistol. This became the **P9**, which, with its variant the **P9S**, has been widely adopted by police and military forces.

The roller delay system resembles, to some degree, the roller locked system used by the Czech CZ52 pistol and can trace its history back to an experimental Mauser rifle of 1945 and possibly back further than that. The rear of the slide contains a two-part bolt separated by two rollers. When the slide is forward, these rollers are forced outwards into recesses in the barrel extension, so locking slide and barrel together. After firing, the cartridge case pushes back on the bolt head; inclined faces on the head then

force the rollers out of the recesses, and due to the angle of the inclined faces this is done at some mechanical disadvantage, causing a delay long enough for the bullet to leave the muzzle. Once the rollers come free, the case can thrust back the bolt and slide to operate the usual cycle of recoil and reloading.

There is an internal hammer, the position of which is shown by an indicator pin at the rear of the slide and this is connected to a de-cocking lever

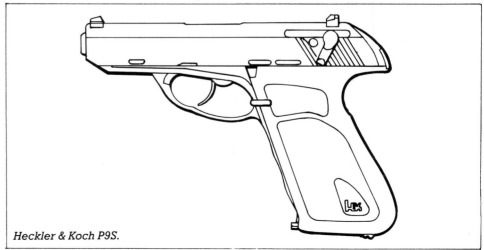

Heckler & Koch P9S.

26

which allows the hammer to be lowered safely on to a loaded chamber. Firing can then be done by using the double action trigger to cock and release the hammer by a straight pull. Subsequent rounds are, of course, fired in single-action mode.

The **P9S** is as described, with double-action. The **P9** was the original model with single-action only, and this was fairly quickly superseded by the **P9S**. In addition to the standard 9mm Parabellum calibre, the pistols were also made in 7·65mm Parabellum and ·45 ACP chambering; the 7·65mm model was dropped several years ago for lack of demand, but the ·45 ACP version has proved popular in the USA.

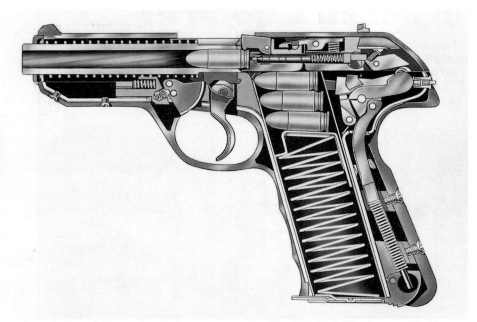

A sectioned view of the mechanical arrangements of the P9 pistol. The two-part bolt can be seen, though the locking rollers are not visible in this view. The P9 is similar to the P9S in general appearance but was single-action only and had a smaller trigger-guard.

Specification:
Calibre: 9mm Parabellum
Operation: Delayed blowback, semi-automatic
Length overall: 192mm
Weight, empty: 880g
Barrel: 102mm, polygonal
Magazine: 9-round box
Muzzle velocity: 350 m/sec

***Manufacturer: Heckler & Koch
GmbH, Oberndorf/Neckar
(Variant Models: P7M8, P7M13,
P7M45, P7K3, P7PT)***

In the middle 1970s the German Federal Police Office issued a specification demanding a pistol of about 9mm calibre, a minimum muzzle energy of 500 Joules, a minimum muzzle velocity of 350 metres per second, and a minimum magazine capacity of six shots. It was to weigh no more than 1kg, be no more than 180mm long and have a barrel of eight to ten calibres length. Most importantly the first shot had to be fired without the need to operate any form of safety catch or lock and the pistol had to be safe against any form of accidental discharge.

This was a stiff bill to meet, and only a handful of makers bothered to try it. Among them was Heckler & Koch with their **PSP** (Polizei Selbstlade Pistole), which was so successful that it was adopted by several German police and security forces as the **'Pistole 7'**, after which H&K renamed it the **P7**.

The basic **P7** has two unique features. Firstly it is a delayed blowback in which the delay is provided by a

piston, connected to the slide, acting inside a cylinder in the frame. Propellant gas passes into this cylinder on firing and resists the rearward movement of the piston due to the recoil of the slide. The second unusual feature is the 'squeeze-cocking' system employed; the front of the grip is a movable bar which is instinctively squeezed inwards when the butt is grasped. This squeezing movement cocks the firing pin, and pressure on

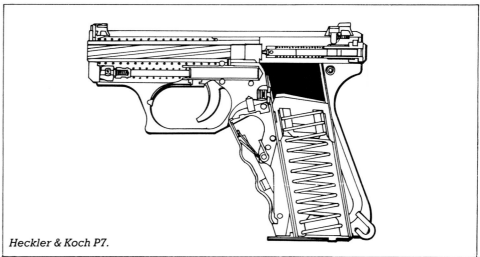

Heckler & Koch P7.

the trigger can then release it to fire the pistol. As soon as the grip is released, the firing pin is uncocked, so there is no need for a safety catch.

The **P7** is now available in a number of forms; the **P7M13** is the standard weapon; the **P7M8** has a more slender butt and an eight-round magazine. The **P7K3** is a simple blowback, but retains the squeeze-cocking feature and is available with interchangeable barrels and other parts, allowing the choice of ·22, 7·65mm ACP and 9mm Short calibres. The **P7PT** resembles the **P7M13** but is designed solely for use with plastic-bullet training ammunition.

The Heckler & Koch P7M10 showing the odd-shaped magazine which reduces a double column to a single feed for reliability. The drawing (left) shows the mechanism of the grip-cocking device, which ensures that should the weapon be dropped it will be in a safe condition before it reaches the ground.

Specification:
Calibre: 9mm Parabellum
Operation: Delayed blowback, semi-automatic
Length overall: 171mm
Weight, empty: 800g
Barrel: 105mm, polygonal, right-hand twist
Magazine: 13-round box
Muzzle velocity: 350 m/sec.

WALTHER MODEL PP

Germany

Manufacturer: Carl Walther GmbH, Ulm/Donau, Germany

This pistol, which appeared in 1929, was the first successful application of the double-action principle to an automatic pistol. Hitherto it had been necessary to load and cock the pistol and carry it cocked, relying on the safety catch, or carry it empty and cock it when the need arose – something not always convenient for police and military users. The double-action system of the **Walther PP** allowed the pistol to be loaded, leaving the hammer cocked as usual. Applying the safety catch then retracted or locked the firing pin and then allowed the hammer to drop safely into the uncocked position. When the need arose, the firer merely had to release the safety catch and pull the trigger to lift and drop the hammer and fire the pistol; after that, the action of the slide cocked the hammer and subsequent shots were fired in the usual single-action mode. For those who required greater precision in the first shot, and who had the time, it was easy to thumb-cock the hammer and fire the first shot in single-action mode; this demands less effort on the trigger and delivers better accuracy.

PP stands for **'Polizei Pistole'** and the weapon was intended to be a holster weapon for uniformed police officers, though it was also widely sold for private use. It appeared first in 7·65mm calibre but was later made in ·22 rimfire, 6·35mm and 9mm Short calibres, though these are less common than the 7·65mm version.

A simple blowback weapon of sound design and excellent manufacture, the **PP** popularised the idea of a 'loaded

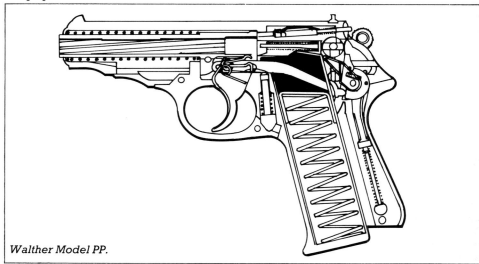

Walther Model PP.

30

chamber indicator', a small pin which protrudes from the rear of the slide when a cartridge is loaded, a signal which can be seen, or felt in the dark. During World War Two the **PP** was widely used as a military pistol, particularly by the Luftwaffe. After the war the patents covering aspects of its design were still valid and Walther licensed them to the French firm Manurhin, who made the pistols for several years. Manufacture then returned to Walther and it is still in production, 64 years after its debut. After the expiry of the patents (and before, in some cases) the design was widely copied in several countries, and a number of East European pistols appear to have drawn their inspiration from the PP.

A pre-war model of the Walther PP, with the original Zella Mehlis address engraved on the slide. The first successful double-action automatic, the PP ushered in a new era of streamlined, simple but reliable pistols and this model was widely used by German police forces and adopted by the Luftwaffe.

Specification:
Calibre: ·22RF, 6·35mm, 7·65mm, 9mm Short
Operation: Blowback, semi-automatic
Length overall: 162mm
Weight, empty: 710g
Barrel: 85mm, 6 grooves, right-hand twist
Magazine: 8-round box
Muzzle velocity: 290 m/sec. (7·65mm)

WALTHER Model PPK

Germany

Manufacturer: Carl Walther GmbH, Ulm/Donau, Germany (Variant Models: PPK/S, TPH)

The Model PP was an immediate success, and was widely adopted by police forces throughout Europe during the 1930s. This led to a demand from plain-clothes police officers for a smaller version which could be more readily concealed about the person, and Walther developed the **Model PPK – 'Polizei Pistole Kriminal'** – ie, a pistol for the 'Kripo' or Kriminal Polizei, the detective branch of the German police forces.

The **PPK** appeared in late 1931 and was a smaller version of the PP, the overall length and height being reduced and the capacity of the magazine similarly cut down to fit the new dimensions. The double-action trigger mechanism and safety arrangements remained the same, but the actual construction of the pistol frame was considerably changed. In the PP the butt was a shaped steel outline with screwed-on grip plates. In the **PPK** the butt was a simple rectangular framework and the grip was an all-enveloping plastic moulding which provided the rear shaping to fit the hand. In addition, since the butt was rather short, the magazine was fitted with a small plastic spur at the bottom, which acted as a convenient rest for the firer's little finger.

As with the PP, the **PPK** was a great success and was widely adopted. It, too, was manufactured by Manurhin after the war before returning to the Walther factory where it is still manufactured. It has not been copied to such an extent as the Model PP.

In the 1960s the **PPK** became very popular in the USA as an off-duty pistol for police officers, but the Gun Control Act of 1968 laid down a minimum depth of four inches for imported pistols; since the **PPK** measured 3·9 inches from top of slide to bottom of butt, this cut it out of a lucrative market. Walther therefore developed the **PPK/S** especially for the USA: this is virtually the frame of the PP carrying the slide and barrel of the PPK; while the length remained the same, the depth increased to 4·1 inches and thus became legally acceptable.

A further variation is the **Model TPH**,

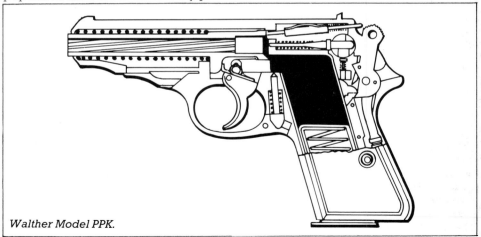

Walther Model PPK.

which is virtually a scaled-down **PPK** chambered for either the ·22 rimfire or 6·35mm cartridges. Introduced in 1968 this is only 135mm long and is an excellent 'vest pocket pistol' though it has little military or police application due to the small cartridge.

The model TPH is a smaller version of the PPK, this version being the ·22 calibre model.

The PPK was a reduced C-scale model of the PP intended for use by plain-clothes police. The mechanism was the same, and it fired the same range of cartridges, but there was a minor difference in the construction of the grip frame. This is another pre-1945 weapon made at the company's original Zella Mehlis factory.

Specification:
Calibre: ·22RF, 6·35mm, 7·65mm, 9mm Short
Operation: Blowback, semi-automatic
Weight, empty: 590g
Barrel: 80mm, 6 grooves, right-hand twist
Magazine: 7-round box
Muzzle velocity: 290 m/sec. (7·65mm)

WALTHER P38 Germany

Manufacturer: Carl Walther GmbH and others

The German Army adopted the Parabellum (Luger) in 1908 and it served them very well; but in the mid 1930s they decided that a more modern design which would be easier and cheaper to manufacture should replace it, and called for suggestions. Walther replied by producing an enlarged version of the PP in 9mm Parabellum, but the Germany Army would not accept a blowback pistol in that calibre.

Walther's next attempt was a locked breech pistol using an internal hammer; this was refused on the grounds that invisible hammers could be cocked or uncocked and nobody could tell which. Finally Walther produced their 'Heeres Pistole' with locked breech and visible hammer, and this was accepted by the Army, who adopted it as their **'Pisole 38'** in 1938.

The **P38** had an exposed barrel which carried a locking wedge beneath it; when the pistol was ready to fire this wedge locked the barrel and slide together. On firing, barrel and slide recoiled a short distance, and then the wedge was cammed down to unlock it from the slide and halt the barrel. The slide continued rearwards to extract and eject the spent case and cock the hammer, then returned to chamber a new cartridge and, pushing the barrel forward, lifted the lug to re-lock the breech.

In addition, the double-action trigger and drop-hammer safety catch of the Models PP and PPK was carried over into the **P38**, making it the first military-calibre pistol to use the double-action

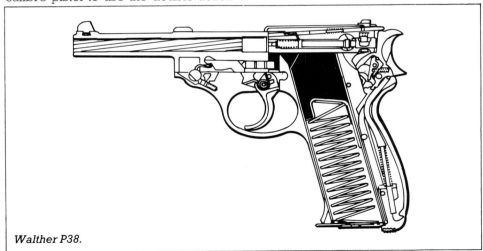

Walther P38.

34

trigger system. The 'loaded chamber indicator' was also adopted.

Although it proved to be very little cheaper than the Parabellum, the **P38** was certainly easier and quicker to manufacture, but wartime demands were too much for Walther and other companies also made the **P38**, while smaller firms made various components.

Walther resumed production of the **P38** in 1957 and it was re-adopted by the Bundeswehr as the **'Pistole 1'**. It has also been adopted by other military and police forces. A short-barrel version, the **P38K** was developed in the mid-1970s; this had the barrel cut down and the front sight mounted on the front end of the slide. Another shortened version was the **P4**, with a barrel length midway between the **P38** and **P38K**. Neither stayed in production for very long.

The Walther P38K was a shortened version of the P38 intended as a heavy-calibre police weapon, but although a perfectly sound gun it did not meet the modern safety requirements demanded by the German police in the 1970s and was therefore replaced by the P5.

Specification:
Calibre: 9mm Parabellum
Operation: Short recoil, semi-automatic
Length overall: 213mm
Weight, empty: 960g
Barrel: 127mm, 6 grooves, right-hand twist
Magazine: 8-round box
Muzzle velocity: 350 m/sec.

***Manufacturer: Carl Walther GmbH,
Ulm/Donau, Germany
(Variant Models: P5 Compact;
P1A1)***

Like many other European designs, the inspiration for the **P5** came from a demand by the German Federal Police Office for a new pistol in the middle 1970s. They demanded double-action triggers, large capacity magazines, and the minimum of preparation before opening fire, and this led to a complete new generation of weapons.
The **P5** is an updated version of the P38 design. It uses the same method of breech locking, the same trigger mechanism and generally resembles the P38 except that instead of the familiar protruding barrel and open-topped slide it has a short barrel and an all-enveloping slide which is similar to most other automatic pistols.
The safety system, however, was drastically revised in order to meet the police requirements. The safety catch was moved to the left side of the frame and has become primarily a de-cocking lever with safety functions as a by-product. The safety of the weapon is provided by an automatic system built in to the firing pin area. The firing

pin is normally out of line, the rear end being pressed down by a spring so that the rear end of the firing pin lies opposite a recessed section of the pistol's hammer; thus, should the hammer fall for any reason the recessed part will enclose the firing pin end, and the bulk of the hammer will strike the body of the slide. When the trigger is pressed, a trip lever on the hammer mechanism is actuated, and this lifts the firing pin against the spring pressure and aligns it properly

with the striking face of the hammer. Continued pressure on the trigger releases the hammer to strike the pin, and as soon as the trigger is released the pin is forced back into the safe position.
The **P5** was adopted by a number of German police forces and also by the Netherlands police and Portuguese and other armies.
In 1988 the **P5 Compact** was introduced; this, as the name implies, is a shortened version of the **P5** with the

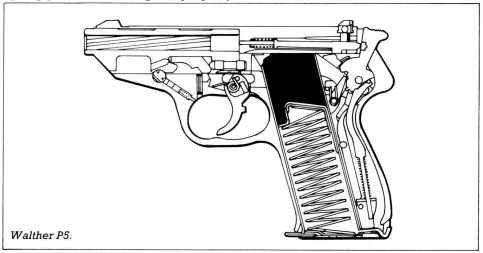

Walther P5.

same mechanical features. The **P1A1** followed this, and is virtually the **P5** but with the addition of a positive cross-bolt safety catch in the slide and with the magazine release placed on the heel of the butt instead of behind the trigger.

The **P5** is also produced in 7·65mm Parabellum and 9x21mm IMI chambering to special order.

The Walther P5 is based upon the same breech locking system as the P38 but incorporates a greatly revised and improved set of safety devices to ensure that the weapon can never be fired inadvertently.

Specification:
Calibre: 9mm Parabellum
Operation: Short recoil, semi-automatic
Length overall: 180mm
Weight, empty: 795g
Barrel: 90mm, 6 grooves, right-hand twist
Magazine: 8-round box
Muzzle velocity: 350 m/sec.

WALTHER P88 Germany

Manufacturer: Carl Walther GmbH, Ulm/Donau, Germany

Although the P5 met with initial success, like all the P38 family it is, by modern standards, a difficult weapon to manufacture due to the method of breech locking which was adopted. Shortly after the P5 went on sale, newer designs from other manufacturers appeared which were less expensive, and sales of the P5 suffered. Walther therefore set about developing an entirely new pistol, the **P88**, which would regain their market position. At present it supplements the P5 series, but will probably replace it in the future.

The **P88** appeared in 1988 and was a completely new design; the dropping wedge lock designed by Barthelmes in the 1930s was finally abandoned and the well-tried Colt/Browning method of locking the barrel to the slide and unlocking it by lowering the breech end by means of a cam was adopted for the first time. Instead of the usual ribs on the barrel locking into recesses in the slide, the chamber area of the barrel is formed into a rectangular shape, and this locks into the rectangular ejection port cut into

the top of the slide; this method is easier to manufacture than the rib system and is also a more positive lock, since guaranteeing complete engagement of the ribs involves very careful fitting.

The trigger mechanism is the familiar Walther double-action, and the firing pin safety system is the same as that used on the P5, in which the pin is held out of alignment with the hammer by a spring until the final movement of the

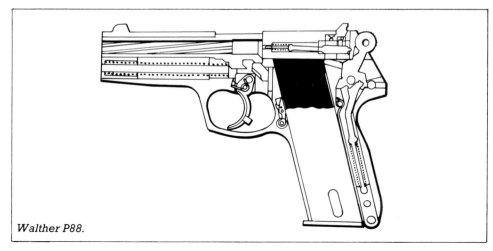

Walther P88.

38

trigger linkage which lifts the pin into position. There is a de-cocking lever on both sides of the pistol which also acts as a slide release lever, and the magazine release button is also duplicated on both sides of the weapon.

The sights are large and well-defined, and the rear sight is mounted on a screw base which allows it to be moved laterally for zeroing adjustment.

In addition to the standard 9mm Parabellum calibre the **Walther P88** is also available in 9x21mm calibre, a compromise cartridge which has been developed for sales in countries where the standard 9x19mm Parabellum round is prohibited to non-military users. At the time of writing the **P88** is undergoing evaluation by a number of military forces, including the British Army.

Specification:
Calibre: 9mm Parabellum
Operation: Short recoil, semi-automatic
Length overall: 187mm
Weight, empty: 900g
Barrel: 102mm, 6 grooves, right-hand twist
Magazine: 15-round box
Muzzle velocity: 350 m/sec.

The P88 is a considerable departure from earlier Walther designs, using a modified Browning tilting barrel to lock the breech. In the summer of 1993 a compact version was announced, with a 97mm barrel and 14-round magazine capacity.

FÉG P9 Hungary

Manufacturer: Fegyver és Gazkeszuelekgyara, Budapest (Variant Models: P9R; P9RA; FP9)

FÉG (the initials of a title which translates to 'Arms and Gas Appliances Factory') in their **P9** series merely took the Browning GP-35 High-Power as it stood and copied it. There are some slight dimensional differences here and there, but in spite of this a high proportion of **FÉG** and Browning pieces are interchangeable. After this **FÉG** went on to introduce some improvements of their own and the variant models exhibit some interesting differences.

There is, therefore, no need to explain the **P9** in great detail, since it simply duplicates the Browning GP-35. The first change to appear in the basic design was the adoption of a slide-mounted safety catch replacing the original frame-mounted pattern. This became the **P9R** and replaced the original **P9** in production in the early 1980s. With it came the **P9RA** which has a light alloy frame, reducing the empty weight to 820 grammes. Both these weapons were provided with double-action triggers, a notable change from the original Browning design, and with ventilated sight ribs over the slide. The slide-mounted safety catch also acts as a de-cocking lever, lowering the hammer when applied and placing a positive block between the hammer and the safety pin; this mechanism has several affinities with that of the Walther P-38 pistol safety system. An interesting variation on the **P9R** is the availability of a completely left-handed version in which the safety catch, magazine release and slide stop lever are on the right side of the frame and the ejection port lies on the left side of the slide.

The original **P9** is now known as the **FP9**, the principal change being a slight deepening of the frame in front of the trigger-guard and the addition of a ventilated sight rib. So far as is known no military force uses the **P9** pistol, though it is believed that some European police forces have adopted them.

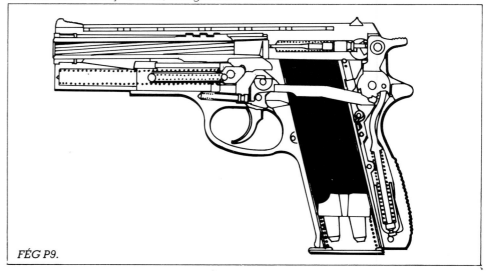

FÉG P9.

The FÉG P9 stripped for cleaning and showing its similarity to the Browning GP-35 design.

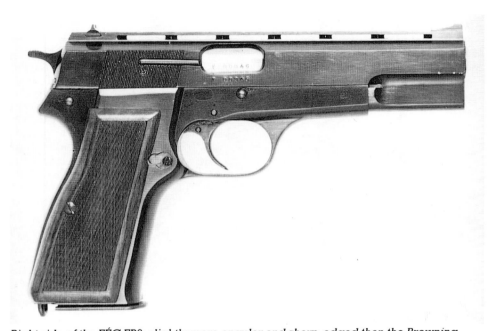

Right side of the FÉG FP9; slightly more angular and sharp-edged than the Browning GP-35, it also differs in having a ventilated rib on top of the slide, intended to prevent heat haze interfering with the sight line.

Specification:
Calibre: 9mm Parabellum
Operation: Short recoil, semi-automatic
Length: 203mm
Weight, empty: 1000g
Barrel: 118·5mm, 6 grooves, right-hand twist, one turn in 250mm
Magazine: 14-round box
Muzzle velocity: 350 m/sec

DESERT EAGLE

Manufacturer: Ta'as Israel Industries, Ramat Hasharon

The **Desert Eagle** pistol was originally developed for long range target shooting and 'silhouette' shooting, but it has since been adopted by one or two Special Forces who require this particular type of firepower. It is a big, heavy pistol firing a powerful round, but it is not so grotesque as many specialised super-pistols and, with the proper cartridge, can be handled as well as most smaller pistols.

It can trace its ancestry back to the same Scandinavian design which fathered the Wildey gas-operated pistol, though the method of utilising the propellant gas to operate the **Desert Eagle** is much different to that of the Wildey. Both, however, use similar methods of locking the breech, a rotating bolt which is turned by a cam reacting with a stud fixed in the moving slide; the first rearward movement of the slide will rotate the bolt lock sufficient to unlock it, after which further slide movement draws the bolt back to extract and eject the spent case.

The gas action is provided by a short-stroke piston set in the frame beneath the barrel. In order to obtain a degree of delay before the piston moves, the gas port in front of the chamber directs the gas through a channel in the frame until it is almost beneath the muzzle; the gas is then directed downwards and back into the gas cylinder, where it strikes the piston. This strikes the forward part of the slide, which extends alongside and below the barrel and it drives the slide

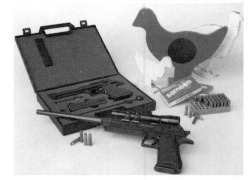

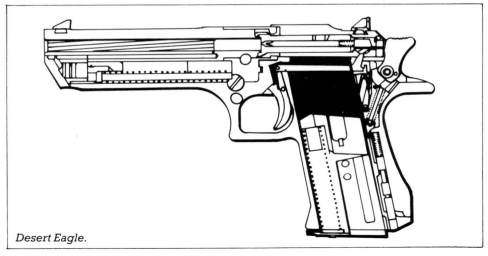

Desert Eagle.

backwards to start the unlocking of the breech. It will be seen that without the long and tortuous path of the gas channel, the breech would be likely to open far too quickly for safety; the alternative to this would be to make the moving parts a good deal heavier.

The **Desert Eagle** was unusual in being developed to fire a revolver cartridge, the ·357 Magnum. This choice was dictated by the desire to have a very powerful round which was easily obtainable almost anywhere in the world. The gun was later developed in ·44 Magnum calibre, making it rather more of a handful to control, and in 1989 it was announced that it would be made in ·41 Action Express calibre. This, it appears, was not enough for the seekers after the utmost power, and in 1992 it appeared chambered for the ·50 Action Express cartridge.

Specification:
Calibre: ·357 Magnum, ·44 Magnum, ·41 AE, ·50 AE
Operation: Gas, semi-automatic
Weight: 1·76kg
Length: 260mm
Barrel: 152mm, 6 grooves, right-hand twist
Magazine: 9-round magazine
Muzzle velocity: 450 m/sec.

The Desert Eagle is a large and powerful pistol for long-range shooting; the upper surface of the barrel is grooved to mount a telescope sight and the iron sights can be either plain combat type or adjustable target pattern.

Manufacturer: Ta'as Israel Industries, Ramat Hasharon

Although from the same stable as the Desert Eagle this is a much different weapon, being aimed more at the military and security markets than the competition shooter. It is a conventional recoil-operated semi-automatic pistol, using a cam-dropped barrel to lock the breech; in fact it is more or less the CZ75 pistol as built by the Italian firm of Tanfoglio, reworked to give it a family resemblance to the Desert Eagle. Manufacture is divided between Tanfoglio and Ta'as Industries. The slide runs on rails inside the frame, a more expensive method of construction but one which is generally considered to give far better support to the slide and improve the accuracy of the pistol. The slide-mounted safety catch also acts as a de-cocking lever, and drops the hammer on to the locked firing pin when depressed. The safety catch is duplicated, so that it can be applied by either hand. Unusually for a modern design, there is no form of automatic firing pin safety system.

The **Jericho** is called the '941 Model' because of its unusual ability to change from 9mm to ·41 calibre very quickly. This combination has been chosen because the rim diameter of both cartridges is the same, so that only the barrel and magazine need to be changed to suit the new calibre. Replacement barrel, return spring and magazines are supplied with the pistol, and changing calibre is simply a matter of field-stripping the pistol and then re-assembling it with the replacement parts. The relevant parts are all colour-coded so that there is little risk of inadvertently assembling the wrong units.

The sights are the usual blade foresight and square notch rearsight; but, instead of the usual dots of white paint for use in poor light they are actually fitted with Tritium light inserts which give an excellent night sight picture, and one which will not fade away as the paint wears off. Both front and rear sights can be laterally adjusted.

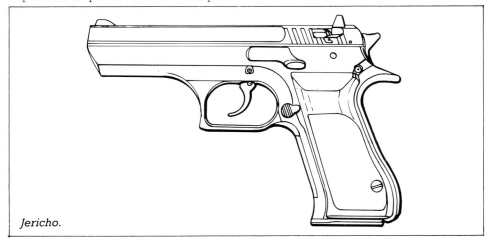

Jericho.

Specification:
Calibre: 9mm Parabellum or ·41 AE
Operation: Short recoil, semi-automatic
Length overall: 207mm
Weight, empty: 1·103kg
Barrel: 112mm, 6 grooves right-hand twist
Magazine: 16-round box (11-round in
·41 calibre)
Muzzle velocity: 350 m/sec.

Although the Jericho resembles the Desert Eagle, its mechanism is more conventional, using the familiar Browning tilting barrel to lock the breech.

The Jericho stripped into its basic parts for cleaning, with both the 9mm and ·41 barrels and their return springs.

45

UZI PISTOL   Israel

**Manufacturer: Ta'as Israel
Industries, Ramat Hasharon**

The Uzi submachine gun is one of the
classic designs, and well-known
throughout the world. In the early
1980s the manufacturers decided to
bow to the current fashion and make it
somewhat more compact, developing
the 'Mini-Uzi' and later the 'Micro-Uzi'.
Inevitably, the question of firing these
smaller weapons one-handed arose,
and from that came the idea of turning
the Mini-Uzi into a semi-automatic
pistol.

Turning a submachine gun into a pistol
involves a certain amount of re-design
so that ill-intentioned people cannot
turn it back into a submachine gun, and
the interior of the **Uzi pistol** is
considerably different to that of its
ancestors. In the submachine gun the
firing pin is a fixture in the bolt and fires
the cartridge as the bolt is closing; in
the pistol the firing pin is a separate
unit attached to a plate at the rear of the
bolt, so that as the block closes the
plate is caught by the sear of the firing
mechanism and held back against the
pressure of the firing pin spring. The
Uzi bolt is, like that of the submachine
gun, a 'telescoped' bolt; the face of the

bolt is recessed so that when closed,
half the bolt is surrounding the barrel.
This enables the action to be shorter
and more compact, while allowing the
bolt to have the amount of weight
necessary to resist the rearward thrust
of the cartridge when it fires; for the
Uzi pistol is a blowback weapon –
there is no bolt lock other than the
bolt's inertia.

The magazine fits into the pistol grip
and, due to the 'telescoped bolt'
design, this is the centre of balance, so
that the pistol handles well in firing,
though it is heavy. The standard

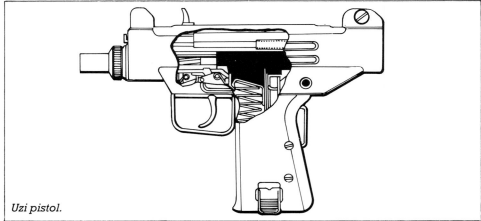

Uzi pistol.

46

magazine holds 20 rounds and, if desired, can be replaced by the submachine gun magazines which hold 25 or 32 rounds.

The sights are fully adjustable and have white reflective markers to assist aiming in poor light. Although appearances may be against it, the Uzi is quite capable of putting all its shots inside a 60mm circle at 25m range; this may not be Olympic standard but it is certainly good enough for military and security operations. And it is a good deal more robust than most pistols.

The Uzi pistol resembles the Uzi submachine gun but cannot be converted to automatic fire. The location of the magazine and butt at the point of balance makes it very easy to fire, in spite of its size and weight. The drawing (left) shows the pistol cocked, and shows the overhung element of the bolt above the chamber.

Specification:
Calibre: 9mm Parabellum
Operation: Blowback, semi-automatic
Weight: 1·81 kg
Length: 242mm
Barrel: 115mm, 4 grooves, right-hand twist
Magazine: 20-round box
Muzzle velocity: 335 m/sec.

BERETTA Model 951   Italy

**Manufacturer: Pietro Beretta SpA,
Gardone Val Trompia**

The Beretta company have made
pistols for the Italian armed forces
since 1915, all of which were simple
blowback weapons firing the 7·65mm
ACP or 9mm Short cartridges. In their
postwar re-organisation the Italian
Army decided they wanted a more
powerful weapon firing the near-
universal 9mm Parabellum cartridge,
and the **Beretta Model 951** was the
result. Design work began in 1950 but
was delayed because of a praise-
worthy attempt to lighten the weapon
by making the frame of light alloy. The
result was a weapon which worked but
which was unpleasant to shoot since
the light weight resulted in an
unacceptable level of recoil, and which
had a potentially limited life since the
force of the recoiling slide tended to
damage the light frame. Eventually the
design was re-worked with a steel
frame; the additional weight made the
weapon more controllable and the
stronger metal precluded damage.
The final version went into Italian
service in 1957, and it was later
adopted by the Israeli Army and
others. It was adopted by Egypt and in

the 1960s a licensed copy, known as
the **'Helwan'**, was manufactured in that
country.

The **Model 951** is recoil-operated
and the breech is locked by a wedge
system similar to that first used in the
Walther P-38. Like almost all Beretta
pistols, the slide is cut away on top so
as to expose most of the barrel, a short
enclosed section at the front
supporting the foresight. The wedge,
which lies beneath the breech, locks
the barrel to the side arms of the slide.
On firing, barrel and slide recoil

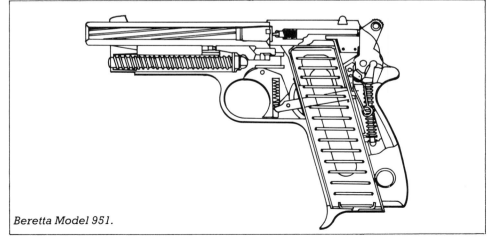

Beretta Model 951.

48

together for a short distance, sufficient time elapsing to allow the bullet to leave the muzzle and breech pressure to drop to a safe level. At that time the wedge, which carries a spring-loaded buffer, strikes a solid part of the frame and is deflected downwards, releasing the slide to continue its rearward movement to extract, eject and re-cock. On the forward stroke the fresh cartridge is loaded and the breech is closed; this forces the barrel forward, lifting the wedge so as to lock once more to the slide.

The trigger action is simple single-action, the weapon needing to be manually cocked before firing by pulling back the slide; the safety catch can then be applied and the pistol carried 'cocked and locked'.

The Model 951 was the first locked breech Beretta pistol and was adopted by the Italian, Egyptian, Israeli and Nigerian armies. Using the Walther P-38 locking block method of closing the breech, it acted as the test-bed for the design which later became the Model 92.

Specification:
Calibre: 9mm Parabellum
Operation: Short recoil, semi-automatic
Length overall: 203mm
Weight, empty: 890g
Barrel: 114mm, 6 grooves, right-hand twist
Magazine: 8-round box
Muzzle velocity: 350 m/sec

BERETTA Model 92

**Manufacturer: Pietro Beretta SpA,
Gardone Val Trompia**

**(Variant Models: 92F, 92F Compact,
92S, 92SB, 92SB-C, 92SB-C Type M,
98, 98F and 99)**

The **Model 92** appeared in 1976 and might be thought of as being the **Model 951** brought up to date. The magazine capacity was increased and the trigger mechanism changed to double-action, but the general shape, the recoil operation and method of locking the breech are exactly the same as that used on the **951**.

The basic **Model 92** has led to a number of variations. Among the first was the **Model 92S**, in which the safety catch was moved from the frame to the slide and given a hammer de-cocking function. Pressing the safety catch releases the hammer after deflecting the firing pin out of the hammer path. Both the **92** and **92S** were adopted by the Italian armed forces and police and widely sold overseas before production ended in about 1986.

In 1980 the US Army sought a replacement for their Colt M1911A1 pistol and Beretta prepared the **Model 92SB** for their tests; this was a 92 with a safety catch on both sides of the slide,

the magazine release in front of the butt, behind the trigger, and an automatic firing pin safety system. The hammer had a half-cock notch and the butt was grooved at the rear to give a better grip. At the same time a 'compact' model, the **92SB-C** was developed, differing only in being smaller. The **Model SB** was successful but the US Army requested some modifications before adopting the design; the modified weapon became the **Model 92F** and the differences were slight. The trigger guard was re-

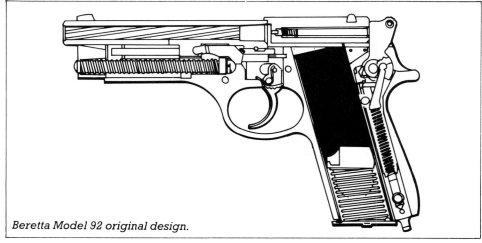

Beretta Model 92 original design.

50

shaped to suit a two-handed grip, the magazine had its base extended, the butt front edge was curved at the toe, and new grip plates and a lanyard ring were fitted. The barrel is chromed internally and the external finish is 'Bruniton', a Teflon-type material. The **92F** was also adopted by the French Gendarmerie and is the current production model.

The other variants can be disposed of fairly rapidly; the **92SB-C Type M** is an **SB-C** with an eight-round magazine; the **92F Compact** is the **92SB-C** with the **92F** modifications; the **98** is a **92SB-C** chambered for the 7·65mm Parabellum cartridge; and the **99** is a **92SB-C Type M** chambered for the 7·65mm Parabellum cartridge.

The Beretta 92 has undergone several changes since the original design shown in the drawing (left); above is the Model 92FS, the latest production version, which equips the US armed forces and Coastguard, the French Gendarmerie Nationale, the Italian Army and other armed forces throughout the world.

Specification:
Calibre: 9mm Parabellum
Operation: Short recoil, semi-automatic
Length overall: 217mm
Weight, empty: 950g
Barrel: 125mm, 6 grooves, right-hand twist, one turn in 250mm
Magazine: 15-round box
Muzzle velocity: 390 m/sec

BERETTA Model 93R   Italy

Manufacturer: Pietro Beretta SpA,
Gardone Val Trompia

Although the **951A** was what the customer wanted, Beretta were not particularly happy with the design and had their own ideas of what a machine pistol ought to be. The principal objection to full-automatic pistols is their unavoidable tendency to muzzle climb due to the recoil force which means that only the first two or three rounds are in the target area. Beretta therefore dropped the full-automatic option and, instead, fitted a three-round burst limiting device. A selector switch on the frame allows the firer to select single shots, in which mode the **93R** is simply a rather larger version of the **92** and acts accordingly.

With the switch set for burst fire, each pressure of the trigger produces three shots at a cyclic rate of about 1100 rounds per minute. This is still rather difficult to control with one hand, so there is a folding forward grip attached to the elongated trigger guard so that the firer can use his free hand to hold the grip, hooking his thumb into the trigger guard, and thus have better directional control.

For even more deliberate firing a collapsible metal butt can be clipped to the end of the pistol's grip and the weapon can then be fired from the shoulder.

To assist in controlling the recoil the barrel is extended and the muzzle is formed into a compensator which also acts as a flash hider when firing at night. Extended magazines are available, giving an increased ammunition reserve; they also add useful weight which helps in

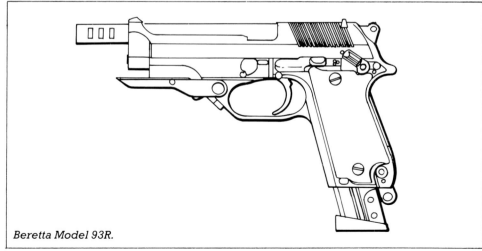

Beretta Model 93R.

controlling the weapon during burst fire.

The **Model 93R** has been adopted by the Italian Special Forces, replacing their earlier **951A** and **951R** models, and has also been purchased by Special Forces of other countries.

The Beretta 93R, showing the forward grip folded up under the frame and the detached metal shoulder stock which can be fitted for additional control. The selector lever on the slide allows single shots, three-round bursts or a safe position, and the muzzle compensator keeps muzzle rise to a minimum.

Specification:
Calibre: 9mm Parabellum
Operation: Short recoil, selective fire
Length overall: 240mm
Weight, empty: 1120g
Barrel: 156mm, 6 grooves, right-hand twist, one turn in 250mm
Magazine: 15-or 20-round box
Cyclic rate: 1100 rds/min
Muzzle velocity: 375 m/sec

***Manufacturer: Lyttleton
Engineering Co., Pretoria***

In the past, South Africa bought pistols from FN, Star and other sources to outfit their armed forces and police, but the UN arms embargo in the late 1960s put a stop to all importation of arms. But instead of emasculating the South African government, as had been intended, the embargo merely turned them inwards and caused them to set up their own armaments industry, so that from being merely a consumer they are now a producer and exporter.

Their first pistol venture was a licence-built design based on the Beretta 92 and known as the Z-88. Once this was into production to fill much-needed gaps in the inventory, the designers set about developing ideas of their own and the **Vektor SP1** is the result.

The **SP1** is a recoil-operated pistol, using a wedge beneath the barrel to lock the slide and barrel together, the system pioneered on the Walther P38 and used in the Beretta 92. This has the advantage of giving the barrel a straight rearward movement and contributes to the accuracy. The slide is machined from solid steel, while the

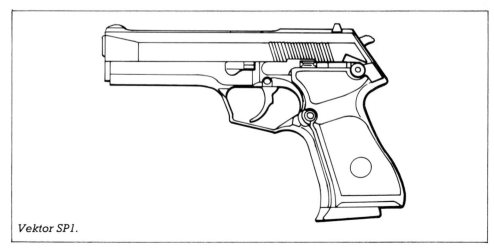

Vektor SP1.

frame is of aluminium alloy. There is an automatic firing pin safety device, preventing firing unless the trigger is fully pulled back, and the pistol can be fired in double- or single-action modes. There is a safety catch on both sides of the frame, and the magazine release can be positioned on either side of the butt to suit the user. Introduced in 1992, the **SP1** is in production for the South African Defence Force and police.

Opposite page (above): the first locally-produced South African pistol was the Vektor Z-88, which, as this view reveals, was little more than a copy of the Beretta 92.

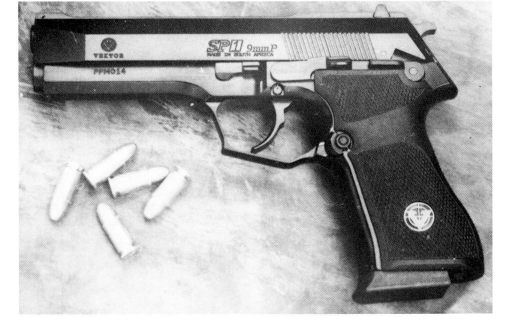

The South African Vektor SP1 is an entirely new design, though the locking system is based upon that of the earlier Z-88.

Specification:
Calibre: 9mm Parabellum
Operation: Short recoil, semi-automatic
Weight: 995g
Length: 210mm
Barrel: 118mm, four grooves, right-hand twist
Magazine: 15-round box
Muzzle velocity: 360 m/sec.

MAKAROV

Manufacturer: State arsenals

The **Makarov** pistol was developed in the early 1950s to replace the Tokarev TT-33 with something simpler to make and easier to shoot. Like all powerful pistols the Tokarev takes some training in order to extract the best from it, but the **Makarov** uses a much less powerful cartridge and is therefore more easily mastered. It became the standard sidearm for all Soviet forces, eventually replaced the Stechkin, and has been exported to many countries who have adopted Soviet weapons.

The design of the **Makarov** is broadly based upon that of the Walther PP, a fixed-barrel blowback semi-automatic with the recoil spring wrapped round the barrel. The trigger is double-action, and the safety catch, which is on the slide, locks the firing pin and lowers the hammer safely on to a loaded chamber when applied. Once this has been done, all that is necessary to fire is to release the safety catch and pull the trigger. This will cock the hammer and then release it to fire the first shot. Subsequent shots will be fired in the single-action mode since the recoiling slide cocks the hammer after each shot.

It can be seen that the shape of the grip is much different to that of the Walther, which makes the **Makarov** somewhat awkward to hold for those accustomed to the PP; stripping is performed in the Walther manner, pulling the trigger guard down and forward to free the slide, after which the slide can be pulled all the way to the rear, the back end lifted clear of the frame, and then the slide can be slid forward, over the barrel, and removed.

The 9x18mm Makarov cartridge was introduced with this pistol and soon became a standard cartridge throughout the Warsaw Pact countries. It is somewhat smaller than the 9mm Parabellum but more powerful than the 9mm Short, so that it is just about at the upper limit of power which can be used in a simple blowback pistol. It is unfortunate that at much the same time the same sort of reasoning led to the development of a similar 9x18mm cartridge in the West; this is the 9mm Police round, which although of the same nominal dimensions is, in fact, very slightly different, so that Western weapons cannot chamber the Makarov cartridge and Soviet pistols cannot fire the 9mm Police round.

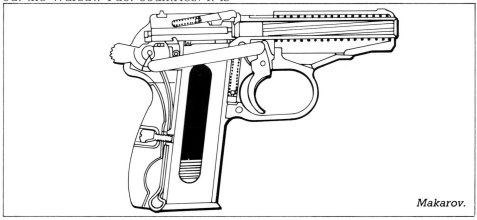

Makarov.

Specification:
Calibre: 9mm Makarov
Operation: Blowback, semi-automatic
Length: 160mm
Weight, empty: 663g
Barrel: 91mm, 4 grooves, right hand twist
Magazine: 8-round box
Muzzle velocity: 315 m/sec

The Makarov became the standard Soviet pistol in the early 1950s and was widely adopted by other Warsaw Pact countries. It fires an unusual 9mm cartridge produced only in Russia and cannot handle western ammunition.

Manufacturer: Unceta y Cia,
Guernica
(Now Astra-Unceta y Cia)
(Variant Model: Astra 600)

The **Astra 400** is that remarkable oddity, a blowback pistol firing a heavy military cartridge. The 9mm Largo cartridge is longer than the 9mm Parabellum and uses a heavier bullet, but the velocity and the muzzle energy are lower. Nevertheless, it delivers considerable recoil and to keep the blowback system under control demanded a heavy return spring and hammer spring to soak up the energy. Cocking the **Astra** requires a very tight grip on the slide to overcome the powerful spring.

Another remarkable feature of this pistol is its ability, when new, to fire a number of different cartridges. It will, when in good condition, chamber and fire the 9mm Browning Long, 9mm Largo, 9mm Steyr and·380 Colt Auto cartridges, and it manages this by a carefully dimensioned chamber and a long firing pin which absorbs small differences in headspace. Once the chamber begins to wear, this tolerance begins to vanish, and with the age of the pistols likely to be found today it is

not a practice to be recommended. The most usual problem arises when attempting to fire 9mm Parabellum in a worn gun; failures to feed often occur, and if they do feed, then they tend to go forward in the chamber so that they are not properly supported by the breech face and blow out their primers.

Production of the **Astra 400** ended in 1946, after some 106,000 had been made. During 1943 an interesting variant model, the **Astra 600,** was made for the German Army; this was a slightly smaller version of the 400 chambered specifically for the 9mm Parabellum cartridge. A total of 10,450 were delivered, after which a further 49,000 or so were made and marketed commercially. A number were supplied to West German police forces in the immediate postwar years.

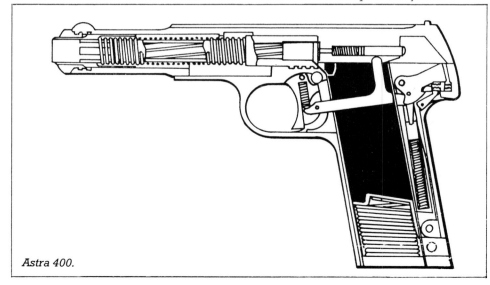

Astra 400.

Specification:
Cartridge: 9x23mm Largo (Bergmann-Bayard)
Operation: Blowback, semi-automatic
Length: 235mm
Weight, empty: 1080g
Barrel: 140mm, 6 grooves, right-hand twist
Magazine capacity: 8 rounds
Muzzle velocity: 345m/sec.

Though it may resemble an air pistol, the Astra 400 was a military weapon firing a powerful cartridge. The design is a modification of the Campo Giro pistol, adopted by the Spanish Army in 1912 and improved by Astra after the death of the inventor in 1915. Astra's design was put into service in 1921, approximately the date of this rare photograph, and was not replaced until the 1950s. The lower photograph shows the Astra 400 with its slide drawn back, showing how the slide fits concentrically around the barrel.

ASTRA A-80 Spain

Manufacturer: Astra-Unceta y Cia, Guernica
(Variant Model: Astra A-90)

The Astra **A-80** is a semi-automatic pistol of modern design, especially adapted for police and military use. Its various features include an advanced double-action mechanism, large magazine capacity, compact size and a choice of popular calibres. The safety system permits carrying the pistol with a loaded chamber without danger of accidental discharge.

On the **A-80** the conventional manual safety catch on the slide is absent. Instead, the pistol has a de-cocking lever which operates in conjunction with the double-action trigger mechanism. Pressure on the de-cocking lever releases the hammer to allow a safety notch to engage with a corresponding notch on the sear, so arresting the hammer's movement before it can strike the firing pin. In addition, a safety block is automatically engaged in recesses in the firing pin, preventing the pin from moving, so that even should the sear fail and the hammer strike the pin, the cartridge will not fire.

The pistol can be fired from the full-cock or uncocked position by a pull of the trigger. In either case, the automatic firing pin safety block is raised, to free the firing pin, by the action of the sear during the final movement of the trigger. As normally supplied the pistol is designed for right-handed users, but a left-handed de-cocking lever and associated components can be provided.

The **A-80** was introduced in 1981 and has been purchased by a number of military and security forces. In 1985 an improved design, the **A-90** was introduced. This is much the same weapon but with the addition of a manual safety catch on the slide which is linked to a new two-piece firing pin. On setting the catch to safe the rear end of the firing pin is tilted so that the rear is concealed from the hammer and the front is no longer aligned with the rest of the pin. The de-cocking lever and automatic firing pin safety of the **A-80** are also present, so giving the user a number of safety options.

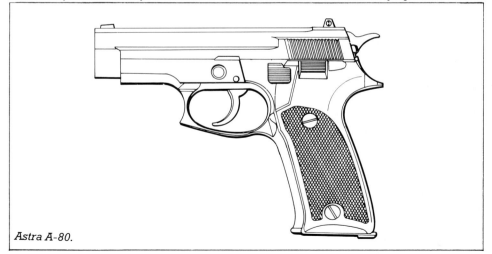

Astra A-80.

Specification:
Calibre: 9mm Parabellum, ·38 Super Auto, ·45 ACP or 7·65mm Parabellum
Operation: Short recoil, semi-automatic
Length: 180mm
Weight, empty: 985g
Barrel: 96·5mm
Magazine: 15-shot box (8-shot in ·45 calibre)
Muzzle velocity: 350 m/sec (9mm Parabellum)

Dismantling the Astra A-80 is done by rotating a locking pin and sliding the two halves of the pistol apart.

Reminiscent of the SIG-Sauer designs, the Astra A-80 uses a de-cocking lever to control its double-action firing mechanism. The later A-90 added a manual safety catch to the slide to give positive control over the firing pin.

LLAMA M82   Spain

Manufacturer: Llama-Gabilondo y Cia, Vitoria

Gabilondo began making cheap revolvers in 1904 and turned to simple automatic pistols during World War One in order to meet French demands. After the war they made copies of Browning pistols and then, in 1931, began producing the **'Llama'** series of automatics, which were among the best of Spanish pistols. These were all external-hammer single-action pistols based on the Colt M1911 design; they were well made and widely exported. The 9mm **'Llama Especial'** model was used by the Nationalist forces in the Spanish Civil War, and after that war Gabilondo were one the three Spanish gunmakers permitted to manufacture pistols (the others being Star-Bonifacio Echeverria and Astra-Unceta).

The **M82** was introduced in the early 1980s and was thereafter adopted by the Spanish Armed forces. It is a modern pistol, with double action trigger, and it moves away from the traditional Llama method of using the Browning lock to adopt a breech locking system relying upon a locking wedge beneath the barrel, the same system as pioneered on the Walther P-38. The wedge locks the barrel and slide together; as the two recoil after firing, so the wedge strikes a spring plunger mounted in the frame and is deflected downwards so as to unlock from the slide. The slide then performs the reloading cycle and is relocked to the barrel after the fresh round has been chambered.

The pistol is loaded in the usual way by setting the slide-mounted safety catch to 'safe' and inserting a magazine, then pulling back the slide and releasing it. As the slide goes forward so the hammer drops safely upon the loaded chamber. The pistol can then be carried, and when required all that is necessary is to push up the safety catch and pull the trigger.

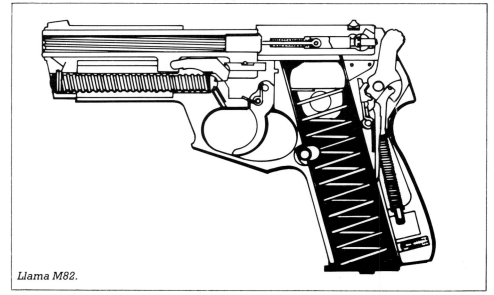

Llama M82.

Specification:

Calibre: 9mm Parabellum
Operation: Short recoil, semi-automatic
Length: 209mm
Weight: 1110g
Barrel: 114mm, 6 grooves, right-hand twist
Magazine: 15-round box
Muzzle velocity: 345 m/sec.

The Llama 82 is the current Spanish Army service pistol, and uses the same breech locking system as the Beretta 92. An unusual feature is that the hammer falls to a safe position after the gun has been loaded and the slide pulled back to load the chamber. It is possible to thumb-cock the hammer, but double-action shooting is the norm.

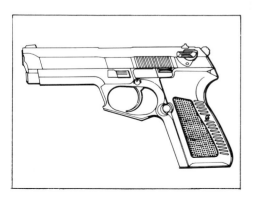

STAR Model 30M   Spain

**Manufacturer: Star Bonifacio
Echeverria SA, Eibar
(Variant Model: 30PK)**

The Star company are a long-established firm who have specialised in automatic pistols since the 1900s and who are one of the only three Spanish pistol makers to have survived the Civil War. In their early days the company appear to have taken Mannlicher as their design stimulus, but in the 1920s they adopted the familiar Colt/Browning pattern and have remained with it ever since.

The **Model 30** was introduced in 1988 and followed a Model 28, being an improvement on it. The design is modern in that it incorporates an automatic firing pin safety and has the safety catch duplicated on both sides of the slide to facilitate use by right- or left-handed firers. The barrel locking system is controlled by a cam beneath the breech end, acting against a pin in the frame to draw the rear end of the barrel down on recoil and so disengage it from the slide. Locking is performed by two ribs on the barrel mating with two recesses in the slide top.

An unusual feature in this pistol is that the slide is formed with an exterior flange which engages in a groove cut in the interior edge of the frame, so that the slide runs inside the frame; this has only previously been seen in Swiss pistols, and whilst it is doubtless more expensive to manufacture, it has the advantage of offering a longer support surface and thus keeping the slide and barrel assembly in more perfect alignment during the recoil stroke, adding to the accuracy of the weapon.

The safety catch, when applied, retracts the firing pin into its housing so that it cannot be struck by the hammer.

Once the safety has been applied it is simply a matter of pulling the trigger to drop the hammer, after which the pistol can be carried in safety. To fire, the safety is released and the trigger pulled through in order to cock and release the hammer for the first shot. The manufacturers also claim that this system allows the firer to practice 'dry firing' with an empty pistol without the danger of damaging the firing pin. There is also a magazine safety system which prevents the trigger operating if the magazine has been removed; in recognition of the fact that some users dislike this device, it has been fitted in

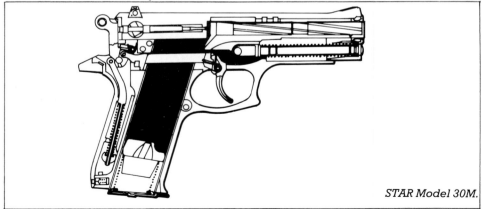

STAR Model 30M.

64

such a manner that the user can remove it if he wishes.

The **Model 30PK** is slightly smaller and has a light alloy frame.

Specification:
Calibre: 9mm Parabellum
Operation: Short recoil, semi-automatic
Weight: 1·14kg (30M); 860g (30PK)
Length: 205mm (30M); 193mm (30PK)
Barrel: 120mm (30M); 98mm (30PK)
Magazine: 15-round box
Muzzle velocity: 375 m/sec.

Standard pistol of the Spanish police services, the Star 30M is unusual in that it is possible to pull the trigger and actuate the hammer even when the safety catch is applied, since this only retracts the firing pin and locks it.
Left: a rear view of the Star 30M, showing the luminous dot sights.

SIG-SAUER P-220 Switzerland

Manufacturer: Schweizerische Industrie Gesellschaft (SIG), Neuhausen-Rheinfalls, J. P. Sauer & Sohn, Eckernförde, Germany

In the early 1970s, doubtless motivated by the various demands for modern automatic pistols which were being made by European police forces faced with increasing terrorism, SIG set out bringing their **P-210** design up to date, making it easier and therefore cheaper to manufacture and also adding some new features.

But no matter how good the pistol might be once put into production, the Swiss laws on the export of firearms had become very stringent, and it was likely that SIG would be unable to sell the weapon outside Switzerland, a market which scarcely made development worthwhile. They therefore set up an arrangement with J. P. Sauer & Sohn, an old-established firearms maker in West Germany, whereby SIG would develop the pistol and Sauer would then make it under license, the German regulations permitting much easier export sales. The result was that the new pistol was introduced as the **SIG-Sauer P-220**.

The **P-220** retains the dropping barrel method of locking the breech, but the method of locking the slide is much simpler; a squared block around the chamber fits into the enlarged ejection port in the side and does the locking. Instead of being machined from raw steel, the new design makes use of investment castings which are then machined on computer-controlled tools.

The trigger is double-action and there is a de-cocking lever on the left side of the frame, allowing the hammer to be lowered safely and then, if desired, cocked for single-action firing. There is an automatic firing pin lock which will only allow the pin to move when the trigger is correctly pulled. In view of these features SIG see no reason to have a manual safety catch on the pistol.

The **P-220** was adopted by the Swiss Army as their **Pistol 75**; it is also used by the Japanese Self-Defence Force and by a number of Special Forces.

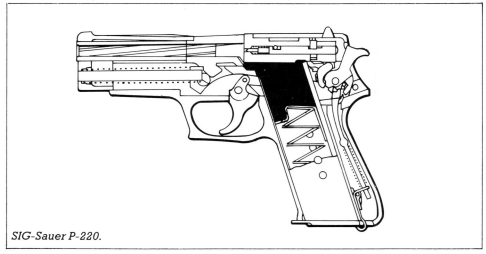

SIG-Sauer P-220.

Specification:
Calibre: 9mm Parabellum
Operation: Short recoil, semi-automatic
Length: 198mm
Weight, empty: 830g
Barrel: 112mm, 6 grooves, right-hand twist
Magazine: 9-round box
Muzzel velocity: 345 m/sec.

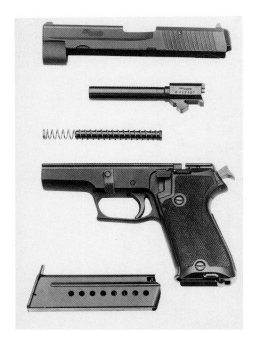

The SIG-Sauer P-220 heralded a new generation of SIG pistols when it appeared in 1974. The locking, by means of the chamber area into the ejection port, was unique, and the de-cocking lever resurrected a design used by Sauer in their 1938 pistol. Adopted by the Swiss and Japanese armies, it is widely used by security forces all over the world.
Left: this view of the SIG-Sauer P-220 dismantled shows the cam beneath the chamber and the shaped area around the chamber which provides the breech locking.

SIG-SAUER P-225　　　　　Switzerland

Manufacturer: Schweizerische Industrie Gesellschaft (SIG), Neuhausen-Rheinfalls, J. P. Sauer & Sohn, Eckernförde, Germany.

The P-220 was a considerable success, and led to requests for something similar but rather smaller, which could be carried concealed. This led to the **SIG-Sauer P-225**, which took the basic design of the P-220 and simply reduced its dimensions and weight. The automatic firing pin safety was improved so that not only did it keep the pistol safe against accidental discharge, it also prevented discharges due to the pistol being dropped or struck whilst cocked.

The **P-225** appeared shortly after the German Federal Police authority had specified various features for a new pistol, and since it complied with most of these requirements it was soon adopted by a number of Swiss and German state police forces. It was also taken into use by the US Secret Service, and a number of Special Forces of different armies have adopted it.

In 1980 the US Army made its requirements for a new pistol known, and SIG saw that with some small modifications the **P-225** could be a likely contender. Using many existing parts of the P-220 and P-225, they developed the **P-226** and submitted it for the US Army trials. The pistol was almost the same size as the P-220 but adopted a larger capacity magazine and an ambidextrous magazine release in order to meet American requirements.

The **P-226** did extremely well in the US trials and was rated a 'technically acceptable finalist'; indeed, it was widely believed that it would be chosen as the US Army's new pistol, arrangements having been made for manufacture in the USA by the Maremont Corporation. However, at the last moment it was beaten on price by the Beretta 92F, which was duly accepted by the US Army. In spite of this setback SIG put the **P-226** into production and it has been adopted by several military and police forces throughout the world.

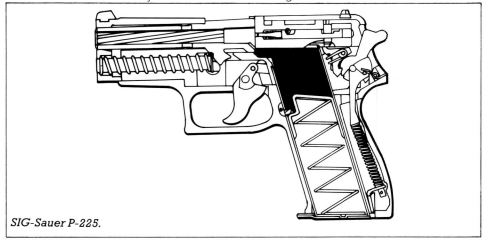

SIG-Sauer P-225.

Specification (P-225):
Calibre: 9mm Parabellum
Operation: Short recoil, semi-automatic
Length: 180mm
Weight, empty: 740g
Barrel: 98mm, 6 grooves, right-hand twist
Magazine: 8-round box
Muzzle velocity: 340 m/sec.

Specification (P-226):
Length: 196mm
Weight, empty: 750g
Barrel: 112mm, 6 grooves, right-hand twist
Magazine: 15-round box
Muzzle velocity: 350 m/sec.

The SIG-Sauer P-225 (above) is a smaller version of the 220 with even more safety devices, so that even if the hammer slips during cocking it remains perfectly safe. There is no safety catch, and operation is as instinctive as that of a revolver. The P-226 (left) is a variant model designed to compete in the US pistol trials of 1981, in which it was narrowly beaten on price by the Beretta 92.

SIG-SAUER P-228/229   Switzerland

Manufacturer: Schweizerische Industrie Gesellschaft (SIG), Neuhausen-Rheinfalls, J. P. Sauer & Sohn, Eckernförde, Germany

The **P-228** was developed in order to provide a compact pistol with a large magazine capacity, thus filling a gap in the SIG product line. A double-action pistol, the **P-228** has a magazine capacity of 13 rounds and has been designed so as to be very resistant to dust and dirt. There is the usual automatic firing pin safety system and a de-cocking lever, and the magazine catch can be mounted on either side, as the user prefers. A large number of the components are the same as those used on the P-225 and P-226 pistols, and most of the accessories for those weapons can be used with the **P-228.**

The **P-229** is virtually the same pistol as the **P-228** but differs in being chambered for the ·40 Smith & Wesson automatic pistol cartridge instead of the 9mm Parabellum round. It has been designed primarily for used by police and security forces, particularly in the USA where the ·40 cartridge has attracted a considerable following.

There are three variant models; the P-229 is the basic version, with steel slide and aluminium frame; the P-229SL is the same but with a stainless steel slide, and this version can also be supplied in 9mm Parabellum calibre.

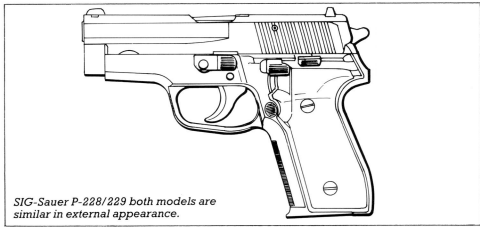

SIG-Sauer P-228/229 both models are similar in external appearance.

Specification (P-228):
Calibre: 9mm Parabellum
Operation: Short recoil, semi-automatic
Length: 180mm
Weight, empty: 830g
Barrel: 98mm, 6 grooves, right-hand twist
Magazine: 13-round box
Muzzle velocity: 340 m/sec.

Specification (P-229):
Calibre: ·40 Smith & Wesson
Operation: Short recoil, semi-automatic
Length: 180mm
Weight, empty: 865g
Barrel: 98mm, 6 grooves, right-hand twist
Magazine: 12-round box
Muzzle velocity: 290 m/sec.

Based on a well-tried design, the P-228 is a compact pistol widely used by security forces and bodyguards in many countries.

SPHINX AT-2000S   Switzerland

**Manufacturer: Sphinx Engineering
SA, Porrentruy
(Variant Models: AT-2000P,
AT-2000H)**

This first appeared in 1984 as the ITM
AT-84 and was simply a licensed copy
of the Czech CZ75 made in
Switzerland. Thereafter the Swiss
licensees made a number of minor
changes and improvements, so that the
present **AT-2000** models can be
considered as individual designs in
their own right.

The barrels are specially made by a
specialist barrel-maker in Germany.
Several parts have been redesigned
so that they are now no longer interchangeable with original CZ75 parts. A
new Swiss-designed automatic firing
pin safety system has been added; this
keeps the firing pin positively locked
against any movement except during
the final stages of trigger pull. As soon
as the trigger is released, the safety
block returns to position and locks the
firing pin. Other improvements include
the duplication of the safety catch and
slide stop lever on both sides of the
frame, and the safety catch operating
system has been changed so that it can
be applied when the hammer is
cocked or uncocked.

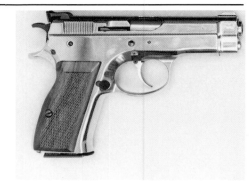

The standard chambering is for 9mm
Parabellum, but the pistol can also be
supplied in 9x21mm calibre for those
countries where 9mm Parabellum is
forbidden to civilian shooters, or in ·40
Smith & Wesson calibre.

The **AT-2000S** is the standard model,
adopted by several police forces and
some military units. The **AT-2000P** is
a compact version, 184mm long and
weighing 940 grams, with all the
features of the **AT-2000S**. The
AT-2000H is the 'Hideaway' version,

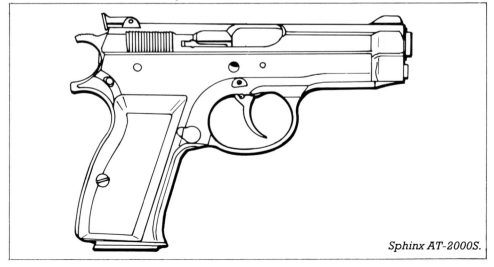

Sphinx AT-2000S.

72

even smaller and with a newly designed barrel and slide, but otherwise retaining all the standard features. As well as the three standard calibres, the **AT-2000H** is also available in 9mm Action Express calibre; this is a cartridge made from the ·41 AE case necked down to take a 9mm bullet, so giving more powder capacity in the case and allowing a higher velocity.

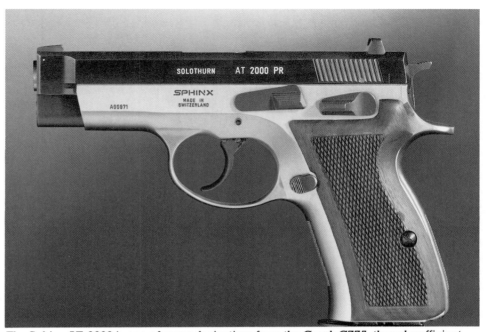

Specification (AT-2000S):
Calibre: 9mm Parabellum, 9x21mm or ·40 S&W
Operation: Short recoil, semi-automatic
Length: 204mm
Weight, empty: 1030g
Barrel: 115mm, 6 grooves, right-hand twist, one turn in 250mm
Magazine: 15-round box (11-round in ·40 calibre)
Muzzle velocity: 352 m/sec.

The Sphinx AT-2000 is one of many derivatives from the Czech CZ75, though sufficient changes have been made to turn it into an entirely new design. This Model PR is the most recent version, has a 'double-action only' firing mechanism, though the hammer can be thumb-cocked if desired.
Left: a stainless steel version of the Sphinx AT-2000S pistol.

CALICO M950   USA

**Manufacturer: Calico Inc.,
Bakersfield, USA**

The **Calico** appeared in 1989 and is a quite unusual weapon; it is modular in construction so that the various parts can be put together so as to produce either pistols or carbines, and the magazine is a tubular component which sits on top of the weapon and has an enormous capacity. Unlike any other pistol, the **Calico M950** feeds from above and ejects the spent cases below.

The frame and receiver unit of the **Calico** is made from cast aluminium and incorporates the butt and also a fore-end which can be grasped by the free hand for better control. The barrel is of chrome molybdenum steel. The bolt mechanism is a delayed blowback design similar to that used in the Heckler & Koch weapons; it consists of two parts, separated by two rollers. On closing, the rear (heavy) section forces the rollers outwards into two recesses formed in the frame. On firing, the rearward thrust on the face of the bolt tries to force the entire bolt assembly rearwards, but movement is prevented because of the engagement of the rollers. The lighter front section of the bolt is allowed a small amount of movement, and this is enough to allow shaped faces to slowly force the rollers inward until they cease to have any locking effect. At that point the entire bolt unit is able to move back under the impetus given to the front section. The bolt travels back in the receiver, extracting and ejecting the empty case and compressing a return spring. A hammer is also cocked during this movement. The spring then returns the bolt, loading a fresh round, and the rollers move out to lock.

The magazine is a cylindrical casing which slides on to the rear of the receiver. Inside it, the cartridges are stacked in two helical layers, and as the rounds feed forward under pressure from a driving spring they roll so as to generate little friction. The standard magazine holds 50 rounds, but a longer magazine holding 100 rounds can also be fitted.

The rear sight is a notch on the magazine, and the front sight forms part of the frame and is fully adjustable for elevation and windage.

Calico M950.

Right: the Calico pistol is an unusual weapon, giving enormous firepower in one hand. This shows the pistol with the 50-round magazine in place, and the 100-round magazine above it.

Left: this drawing of the Calico shows the helical ammunition feed.

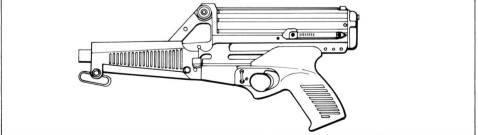

Specification:
Calibre: 9mm Parabellum
Operation: Delayed blowback, semi-automatic
Weight: 1·02kg empty
Length: 355mm with 50-round magazine
Barrel: 152mm, 6 groove, right-hand twist
Magazine: 50- or 100-round helical
Muzzle velocity: 393 m/sec

COLT M1911A1   USA

Manufacturer: Colt Firearms, Hartford, Conn.
(Variant Model: M1911)

This is probably the longest-lived automatic pistol design in military history, having been adopted by the US Army in 1911 and replaced by the Pistol M9 (Beretta 92F) in 1985.

The **Colt M1911** introduced the basic 'swinging link' method of breech locking which has been widely copied. The barrel locks to the slide by means of two lugs on its upper surface engaging in two recesses in the inside of the slide top. When the pistol is ready to fire these lugs are in engagement; the front of the barrel is supported in a bush at the front of the slide, and the rear of the barrel is held up by a vertical hinged link attached to the barrel at its upper end and to the slide stop pin at its lower end. On firing, barrel and slide move backwards due to recoil; as the barrel goes back so it rotates the link about the slide stop pin, and since the link's top moves in an arc, it pulls down the rear end of the barrel, so disengaging the lugs from the slide. Once the barrel is free it stops moving backwards, but the slide continues to move, the extractor pulls the empty case from the chamber and ejects it and the hammer is cocked. A return spring beneath the barrel is compressed, and as this spring expands again so it drives the slide forward to load a fresh cartridge into the chamber and then, again due to the link, swing the rear of the barrel back up and into engagement with the slide. The hammer remains cocked and the pistol is ready to fire again.

Safety is attended to by a manual safety catch on the frame and also by a grip safety, a movable plate let into the rear of the butt. Unless this is properly

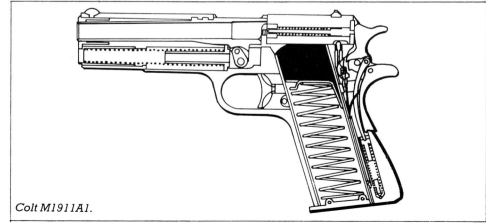

Colt M1911A1.

76

pressed in by the hand gripping the pistol, the weapon cannot be fired.

In the 1920s modifications were made in the light of wartime experience. The rear of the butt was more curved; the front edge of the butt was chamfered behind the trigger; the hammer spur was shortened; and the trigger was made slightly smaller and grooved for a better grip. In this form it became the **M1911A1** in 1926.

The oldest automatic pistol to remain in production, the Colt M1911A1 is essentially unchanged since its debut in 1911 and minor modification in 1926. It uses Browning's original swinging link method of locking the breech (seen in the drawing on the left), and is probably the strongest and most reliable automatic ever made. Even though replaced in US service, it is still widely sold commercially.

Specification:
Calibre: ·45 ACP
Operation: Short recoil, semi-automatic
Length: 216mm
Weight, empty: 1130g
Barrel: 127mm, 6 grooves, left-hand twist, one turn in 406mm
Magazine: 8-round box
Muzzle velocity: 253 m/sec

COLT 2000

**Manufacturer: Colt Manufacturing
Co. Inc., Hartford, Conn., USA**

Although made and sold by Colt, this
was actually designed as a private
venture by Mr. C. Reed Knight and Mr.
Eugene Stoner, after which Colt took
up the design and put it into production
in 1991. It is unusual in that it abandons
John Browning's dropping barrel
system of operation in favour of a
rotating barrel.

The pistol has a steel slide and
polymer frame; the barrel has lugs at
the breech end which engage in
recesses in the slide and a bottom lug
which engages in the cam block;
which, in turn, rests in the frame. The
slide is conventional, having the rear
end formed into the breech block and
carrying a self-cocking striker
mechanism. There is no manual safety
device, the designers aiming at an
automatic pistol which is handled in a
similar way to a revolver.

On firing the recoil drives the barrel
backwards, taking the slide with it, the
breech being securely locked. As the
barrel moves back, so the bottom lug
is drawn through a curved slot in the
cam block, which is held firmly in the
frame. This causes the barrel to turn

through 30° and so release the rear
lugs from the slide. The barrel then
stops and the slide continues rearward
to eject and reload in the usual way.

The trigger mechanism is fitted with
roller bearings to give an exceptionally smooth double-action pull, and
pulling the trigger causes the firing pin
to be first cocked and then released.
An advantage of the cam block design
is that much of the initial recoil shock is
absorbed by the block and transfer of
the shock to the frame is over a greater

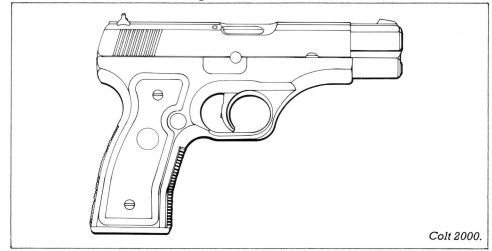

Colt 2000.

area than usual, so producing an unusually low level of felt recoil.

Specification:
Calibre: 9mm Parabellum
Operation: Short recoil, semi-automatic
Length: 190mm
Weight, empty: 822g
Barrel: 114mm, 6 grooves, right-hand twist, one turn in 254mm
Magazine: 15-round box
Muzzle velocity: 350 m/sec

The Colt 2000 departs from the Browning design and introduced a rotating barrel lock. It is also a self-cocking (or 'double-action-only') mechanism using an internal striker instead of an external hammer.
Left: the basic components of the Colt 2000; the 'cam block' is to the left of the trigger assembly.

RUGER P85

USA

***Manufacturer: Sturm, Ruger & Co,
Southport, Connecticut***

Sturm, Ruger & Co came into existence shortly after World War Two, producing an excellent ·22 automatic pistol. Later, when the 'fast draw' craze swept the USA and Colt, ignoring it, failed to put their Single Action Army revolver back into production, Ruger began making single action revolvers, and followed that by modern double-action weapons for police and security use. Rifles and shotguns were added, and finally, in the early 1980s, spurred no doubt by the US Army's demand for a new pistol, development of the **Ruger 85** began. Unfortunately it appeared too late for the US Army's trials, but in spite of that it has met with great success in civilian and police hands.

The **Ruger 85** is in the modern idiom – a double-action pistol with the safety catch and magazine release duplicated on both sides so that it can be used equally easily by right- or left-handed firers. The frame is of light alloy and the remainder of high-grade steel, and extensive use has been made of precision investment casting for the manufacture. Originally located

in New England, the company built a complete new plant with modern computer-controlled machine tools, in Arizona for the manufacture of the **Model 85**.

The slide-mounted safety catch controls both the hammer and the firing pin; moving the catch to the safe position secures the firing pin and then drops the hammer safely. To fire, all that is required is to release the safety and pull the trigger; subsequent shots are in single-action mode. The trigger guard is larger than usual, allowing

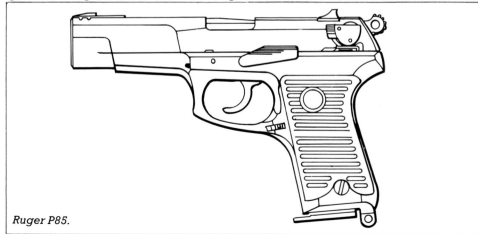

Ruger P85.

easy use by a gloved hand, and the front edge is shaped for a two-handed grip.

The pistol works by short recoil in the usual Colt/Browning way, the barrel being lowered out of contact with the slide by a shaped cam beneath the breech. Instead of the Browning ribs on the barrel, the chamber section is squared off and locks into the ejection opening, a system which is amply strong and which is less troublesome to manufacture than the older rib and recess method.

In late 1989 a variant version, having a single-action trigger mechanism, was put into production for those (and there are many) who prefer their automatics in this form. This was later followed by a version with a de-cocking lever. In 1990, in answer to requests for heavier calibres, the **KP90DAC** model appeared, being the same as the 9mm de-cocker model but in ·45 ACP calibre, and in 1991 the **KP91DAC** chambered for the 10mm Auto cartridge.

Specification:
Calibre: 9mm Parabellum
Operation: Short recoil, semi-automatic
Length: 200mm
Weight: 910g
Barrel: 114mm
Magazine: 15-round box
Muzzle velocity: 354 m/sec.

Arriving just too late for the US Army's pistol trials of the early 1980s, the Ruger P-85 has nevertheless found a place in the commercial market. There are now several variations, in several calibres.
Opposite page: the Ruger P-85 field-stripped to reveal a simple, robust and reliable design.

S&W MODEL 29

**Manufacturer: Smith & Wesson,
Springfield, Mass.
(Variant Model: 629)**

Horace Smith and Daniel Wesson met in the 1850s and as soon as Colt's master patent on revolvers expired in 1857 they went into production with the first breech-loading cartridge revolver, since which time, as they say, the company has never looked back. Their revolvers have always been made to a high standard of finish and are notable for their smooth trigger action. Comparisons with Colt are perhaps inevitable, but in truth there is little to choose between them from the mechanical point of view, one's choice is entirely a matter of personal preference.

The **Model 29** was, for some time, considered to be the most powerful handgun available, and it achieved considerable notoriety in the films of Clint Eastwood. It is a large and heavy weapon, necessarily so since it fired the ·44 Magnum cartridge, propelling a 15·5 gram bullet at 450 metres per second to deliver some 1150 foot-pounds of energy. The recoil from such a load is considerable, even with the weight of the pistol to soak some of

it up, and for many people the ·44 Model 29 is 'too much gun', which eventually led to the development of the ·41 Magnum cartridge and the Model 57 revolver, somewhat less of a handful.

The **Model 29** uses the large 'N' frame and locks the cylinder in place by the usual method of a spring-loaded central pin which anchors it securely to the standing breech and to a shroud formed beneath the barrel to accept the ejector rod. The hammer is chequered on its spur, and the trigger is grooved, both in order to give a non-

slip surface to obviate accidents. The rear sight is adjustable for windage, and the grips are somewhat thicker than usual in order to offer a full bearing surface for the hand and also to prevent the recoil force trapping a finger placed tightly behind the trigger guard or jarring the web of the thumb against the rear of the grip. There are four barrel lengths available – 102, 152, 213 and 260mm – and the pistol can be blued or nickel-plated. The **Model 629** is identical but is made entirely of stainless steel with a satin finish.

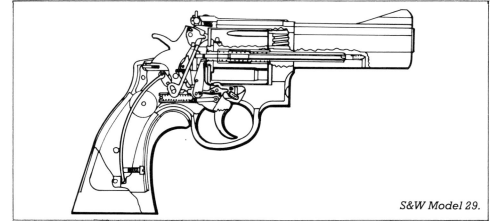

S&W Model 29.

Right: the Smith & Wesson Model 629 in stainless steel and with 4-inch barrel; other barrel lengths are 6·5 and 8·375 inch. With the longest barrel, the pistol weighs 51·5 ounces. The drawing (left) illustrates the robust mechanism, particularly the method of locking the cylinder into the frame.
Below: with the eight-inch barrel, the Model 29 is a lot of gun.

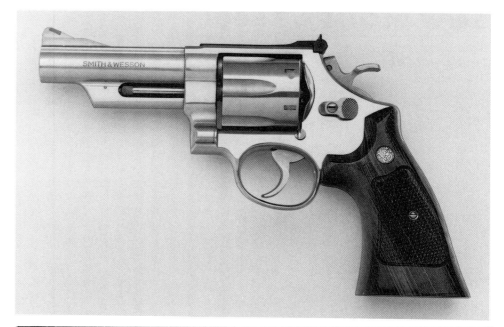

Specification (213mm barrel model):
Calibre: ·44 Magnum
Operation: Double-action revolver
Weight: 1·46kg
Length: 353mm
Barrel: 213mm, 6 grooves, right-hand twist
Magazine: 6-shot cylinder
Muzzle velocity: 450 m/sec.

S&W MODEL 5900

**Manufacturer: Smith & Wesson,
Springfield, Mass.**

Apart from a small pocket pistol in the 1920's, Smith & Wesson did little work on automatic pistols until the early 1950s, when they introduced the Model 39. This was a double-action 9mm automatic using the Colt/Browning system of dropping barrel to lock the breech and slide together. It was provided with a manual safety catch on the slide and used a light alloy frame. It was gradually improved over the years and numbers were adopted by US Special Forces and the US Navy. In 1988 a new series of pistols, the 'Third Generation', was announced. Designed after consultation with many US military and police authorities, this series features such improvements as fixed barrel bushings for better accuracy, a greatly improved trigger-pull, three-dot sights for better aiming in poor visibility, a bevelled magazine aperture to make magazine changing quicker and easier, and improved safety features.

The Model **5900** is the full-sized 9mm Parabellum member of the series; it is accompanied by the mid-sized **3900** and compact **6900** models. The **5900** comes in three forms, the **5903** with alloy frame and steel slide, the **5904** with alloy frame and carbon steel slide, and the entirely stainless **5906**: the other members of the series are similarly subdivided.

The double-action trigger mechanism is fitted with a manual safety and decocking lever mounted on both sides of the slide. This operates in the usual way, safely locking the firing pin before allowing the hammer to drop to the uncocked position. In addition, there is an automatic firing pin safety system in which a spring-loaded plunger positively locks the firing pin except during the final movement of the trigger in firing, when a pawl lifts the plunger and frees the pin to be struck by the falling hammer. Finally there is a magazine interlock safety which prevents the pistol being fired unless the magazine is in place.

The 9mm 5900 series is accompanied by the ·45in Model 4506. This is only

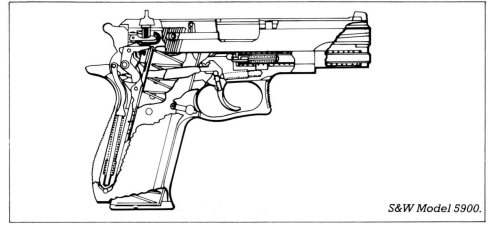

S&W Model 5900.

84

available as a stainless steel model and whilst larger in all dimensions than the 9mm pistols is to exactly the same design with the same features.

Specification:
Calibre: 9mm Parabellum
Operation: Short recoil, semi-automatic
Weight: 737g (Model 5904)
Length: 191mm
Barrel: 102mm, 6 grooves, right-hand twist
Magazine: 14-round box
Muzzle velocity: 350 m/sec.

The Smith & Wesson Model 5904, with alloy frame and steel slide, is representative of the S&W 'Third Generation' automatic models.
Left: the Smith & Wesson Model 1076 is a special 10mm model developed for use by the FBI.

PARKER-HALE MODEL 85

Manufacturer: Gibbs Rifle Co. Inc., Martinsburg, West Virginia, USA

The Parker-Hale company has been famous in the target-shooting world for many years, and the **Model 85** embodies all their experience in a weapon which is widely used by military and police authorities around the world. But in 1990 Parker-Hale sold its rifle business to the Gibbs Rifle Company of the USA, and the **Model 85**, and other Parker-Hale designs, are now manufactured there.

The **Model 85** uses a Mauser-type bolt action. The receiver is a one-piece machined forging into which the heavy barrel is screwed. The barrel is cold-hammered, giving additional strength and a high resistance to wear due to the work-hardening of the interior during the hammering process. It is assembled into the stock so that it is fully-floating, and is bedded into the stock with a special epoxy resin. The muzzle is counterbored to prevent any damage to the rifling when cleaning, and is threaded to accept the foresight block and a sound suppressor.

The bolt has frontal lugs which lock into the chamber, and there is an additional rear lug which, as the bolt is rotated to unlock, moves over a cam surface and eases the bolt back to give primary extraction. The trigger mechanism is a self-contained unit which is secured into the receiver by pins and can be completely removed for cleaning or adjustment. The single-stage trigger is carefully set at the factory for a short and crisp pull, but is fully adjustable by the user.

The safety catch is silent in operation and is of a unique design which positively locks the bolt, trigger and sear. The butt is adjustable for length and a quickly detachable and fully adjustable bipod is fitted to the fore-end. The rifle is fitted with a built-in aperture rear sight, adjustable to 900 metres range, and also has a dovetail to which telescope sights or passive night vision sights may be fitted.

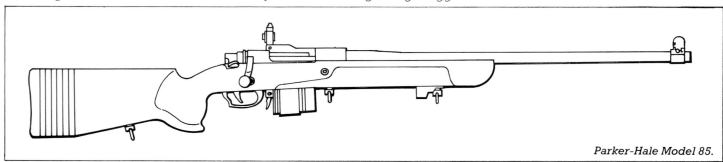

Parker-Hale Model 85.

The Parker-Hale Model 85 is a high-precision sniping rifle, seen here fitted with an electro-optical image intensifying night sight. With selected ammunition it is capable of giving first-round hits at all ranges up to 600 metres.

Specification:

Calibre: 7·62mm NATO
Operation: Manual single shot
Length: 1150-1210mm
Weight, empty: 5·70kg with telescope
sight
Barrel: 700mm, 4 grooves, right-hand twist
Magazine: 10-round box
Muzzle velocity: 860 m/sec.

STEYR AUG

Austria

Manufacturer: Steyr-Mannlicher GmbH, Steyr

AUG stands for 'Armee Universal Gewehr' and comes from the design of the weapon. It is an assault rifle which is constructed from a combination of modules, so that by changing various of these modules it can be configured as a carbine, assault rifle, infantry rifle or light machine gun. It was adopted by the Austrian Army in 1977 and since that time had gone into service in Australia, New Zealand, Ireland,

Morocco, Saudi Arabia, Oman and Indonesia.

The basic rifle consists of a plastic stock into which slides a receiver unit carrying the bolt and gas operating system. The receiver is formed into a carrying handle which encloses a 1·5× optical sight. Into the front of the receiver fits the barrel, which locks in by a part-turn and has a carrying handle and also has a connection to the gas operating system. The transparent plastic magazine fits into the stock,

behind the grip since this is a 'bullpup' rifle with the barrel set well back in the stock so as to allow a full-length barrel in a compact overall size. Finally, the firing mechanism module slides into the rear of the stock and is retained in place by the butt plate.

It will be apparent from this description that changing the barrel is a simple movement, so that any barrel length can be fitted; the longest barrel is also heavier than standard, allowing sustained fire in the machine gun role.

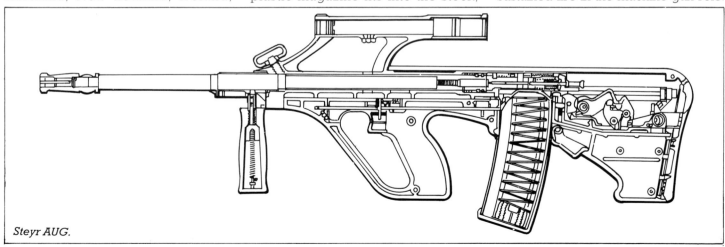

Steyr AUG.

88

The receiver can be changed; instead of one with the carrying handle and optical sight, a receiver with a telescope sight mount can be fitted and thus the user can then fit whatever sight he prefers to use. In standard form the firing mechanism allows single shots or automatic fire, controlled by the trigger; a light pull fires a single shot, but pulling the trigger farther, against an additional spring, gives automatic fire. But the firing mechanism can be exchanged for one giving only single shots, or one which gives single shots and three-round bursts for a single pressure on the trigger. By changing the bolt and switching the ejection port cover to one side or the other, the rifle can easily be suited to right- or left-handed firers.

Steyr AUG is capable of being assembled in varying forms; above left shows the rifle, short rifle, carbine and short carbine variations in 5.56mm calibre. The carrying-handle/sight unit can be changed for a telescope mounting bracket, and the firing mechanism can be changed to provide various choices of single-shot, automatic or burst fire.

Specification:
Calibre: 5·56mm NATO
Operation: Gas, selective fire
Weight: 3·60kg
Length: 790mm
Barrel: 508mm, 6 grooves, right-hand twist
Magazine: 30- or 42-round box
Rate of fire: 650 rds/min.
Muzzle velocity: 975 m/sec.

STEYR ANTI-MATERIAL RIFLE (AMR) Austria

Manufacturer: Steyr-Mannlicher GmbH, Steyr

This rifle was first shown in 1989 and is, at the time of writing, still undergoing final development. It has been designed as a heavyweight precision rifle firing highly specialised ammunition for attacking vulnerable material targets. It can be split in two and carried by two men, and the role envisaged for it is its use by a deep-penetration party that enters enemy territory, take up a position some distance from a forward airstrip, communications centre, radar station, fuel dump or other sensitive and important target and then, by firing a few rounds, inflicts serious material damage to the equipment. The rifle could then be abandoned while the raiders make their escape; one rifle for half-a-dozen expensive aircraft is a good rate of exchange.

The **AMR** is a semi-automatic using the long recoil system of operation. On firing, the bolt and barrel recoil, locked together, for about 25cm. The bolt is then unlocked and held, and the barrel is allowed to run forward again to its rest position. During this movement the empty cartridge case is extracted and ejected. Once the barrel has stopped moving, the bolt is automatically released, to run forward and feed another cartridge into the chamber and then lock.

The cartridge is partly metal and partly plastic and contains a heavy metal flechette, a dart-like projectile much smaller than the 14·5mm calibre. This is surrounded by a 'sabot' which fits tightly in the smoothbore barrel and, pushed on by the propellant gas, carries the flechette down the bore and from the muzzle. Once clear of the

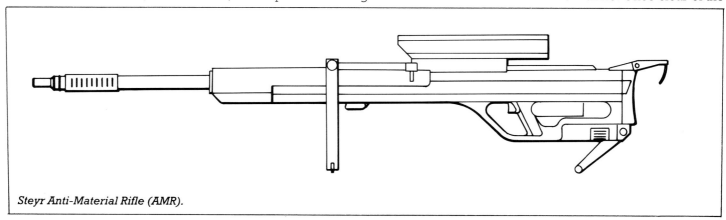

Steyr Anti-Material Rifle (AMR).

muzzle the sabot splits open and air pressure pulls it clear of the metal flechette which continues to the target at high velocity. The flechette can penetrate up to 40mm of steel armour at ranges up to 1000 metres.

The barrel slides inside a cylindrical cradle which contains a hydro-pneumatic recoil system very similar to the sort of mechanism used with artillery. This damps down the recoil and returns the barrel to the firing position; as a result, the recoil felt by the firer is no heavier than might be expected from a heavy calibre game rifle. The rifle is fitted with a 10x telescope sight.

Further development planned for the rifle includes a rifled barrel, so as to give a greater versatility in ammunition design, and the possibility of automatic firing.

Long-range sniping against vulnerable targets is the role of the Steyr Anti-Materiel Rifle, and, depending upon the type of target, it is effective out to 2000 metres range. A recoil-damping cylinder around the barrel reduces the recoil, and the weapon can be quickly dismantled into two loads of man-carrying.

Specification:
Calibre: 14·5mm
Operation: Long recoil, semi-automatic
Weight: 20kg
Length: 2·0m
Barrel: 1·20m, smoothbore
Magazine: 5-round box
Muzzle velocity: 1500 m/sec.

STEYR ADVANCED COMBAT RIFLE   Austria

Manufacturer: Steyr-Mannlicher GmbH, Steyr

In the early 1980s the US Army let it be known that they were searching for a possible design of combat rifle to be adopted some time in the 1990s. Their first move was to set two firms to develop caseless ammunition rifles; then they asked four other manufacturers to develop 'other solutions'. The object was to cover all possibilities by allowing the firms to develop whatever idea they thought best. These designs were all in prototype form by the summer of 1989 and were then put through exhaustive testing by the US Army. Eventually, in 1992, it was announced that none of the competing rifles showed sufficient improvement in performance over the existing M16A2 to make their production worthwhile. Nevertheless, the contest brought out some interesting weapons, and the Steyr design is worth study since even if the US Army did not adopt it, it seems likely to become the Steyr design for the next generation of production weapons.

The rifle has a distinct external resemblance to the AUG, with the same sort of plastic stock, but the mechanism is entirely different. It fires a special plastic-cased cartridge which contains a flechette projectile and the cartridge cap is in the form of a ring around the wall of the cartridge close to the base.

The breech mechanism is entirely novel. The barrel is fixed, and behind it is a chamber block which can move up

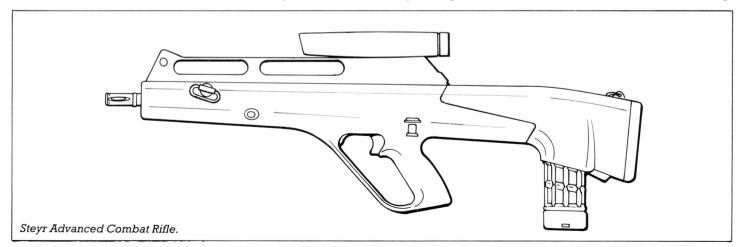

Steyr Advanced Combat Rifle.

92

and down, controlled by an arm driven by a gas piston. This unit also carries a rammer unit. To fire, the cocking handle is pulled back, drawing back the operating arm and rammer. When the trigger is pressed, the rammer flies forward and pushes a cartridge from the magazine into the chamber. The chamber is then released and rises up to line up with the barrel. As it reaches its position a fixed firing pin strikes the annular cap and fires the cartridge, sending the flechette up the barrel. The gas pressure drives the gas piston back, lowering the chamber and repositioning the rammer. The next trigger pressure releases the rammer and as the cartridge is loaded into the chamber so it pushes out the empty case of the previous round, which is ejected forward beneath the barrel.

An optical sight is fitted; it has no adjustment for range since the velocity of the flechette is so high that the trajectory is flat for the weapon's effective range. There is also a shotgun-style rib for quick alignment against moving targets.

Specification:
Calibre: 5·56mm flechette
Operation: Gas, semi-automatic (selective fire)
Length: 765mm

Weight: 3·23kg
Barrel: Smoothbore
Magazine: 24-round box
Muzzle velocity: 1495 m/sec.

The Steyr Advanced Combat Rifle fires a flechette (arrow) projectile at high velocity. The report on the US Army trial said that is was 'the simplest weapon, the simplest round and the most cost-effective approach of any of the contenders'.

STEYR SSG69

Austria

Manufacturer: Steyr-Mannlicher GmbH, Steyr

This was Steyr's first modern military rifle, though 'modern' in this context needs some qualifying. In the early 1960s, when armies were equipping with modern automatic rifles, many of them came to the conclusion that these weapons were not sufficiently accurate for sniping, and the usual solution was to retain some of their old bolt-action weapons for the task. The only problem with that solution was that these bolt-action weapons were, by that time, obsolescent and wearing out. Steyr-Mannlicher saw in this an opportunity to provide a new bolt action of excellent accuracy, using some modern technology.

The **SSG (Scharfschützen Gewehr) 69** was adopted by the Austrian Army in 1969, and this adoption was followed by several others. So far as the mechanical aspect went, the design was fairly conventional, using a turn-bolt action, but the bolt was a new design by Steyr which used six rear lugs to lock the bolt into the receiver. Theoretically, rear lugs are not conducive to accuracy since they allow a degree of compression of the bolt on firing, but by deeply seating the barrel into the receiver Steyr appear to have overcome this. The magazine is the Schoenauer rotary magazine which first appeared in 1887 and, in its perfected form, was used in the Greek Army Mannlicher service rifle of 1903 and in many Mannlicher-Schoenauer sporting rifles and carbines since then. The magazine is a spool which fits neatly into the stock and which can be loaded from a charger; loading the rounds winds up a spring which can then drive the spool to feed cartridges to the bolt. The entire unit can be withdrawn beneath the rifle and has a transparent rear cover which allows the contents to be checked at any time. For those who prefer, a 10-round box magazine can be substituted for the rotary one.

The stock is of plastic material; this was among the first major applications of plastic to a complete rifle stock rather than just butt and fore-end, and proved entirely serviceable; it was doubtless

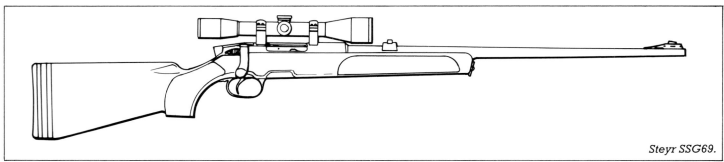

Steyr SSG69.

this experience which led to the plastic stock of the AUG.

The **SSG69** is provided with a conventional V-notch rear sight and blade foresight, but these are solely for emergency use, and the receiver is formed into a mount to which virtually any sighting telescope can be fitted. The rifle is normally supplied with a Kahles ZF69 sighting telescope of 6x magnification, graduated up to 800 metres.

The Steyr SSG69 sniping rifle: (top) Police model with only telescope sight; (below) Standard, with iron and telescope sights; (below) Suppressed model with built-in silencer; (bottom) Special model with short barrel and flash hider.

Specification:
Calibre: 7·62mm NATO
Operation: Manual, single-shot
Length: 1140mm
Weight, empty: 3·9kg
Barrel: 650mm, 4 grooves, right-hand twist
Magazine: 5-round rotary or 10-round box
Muzzle velocity: 860 m/sec.

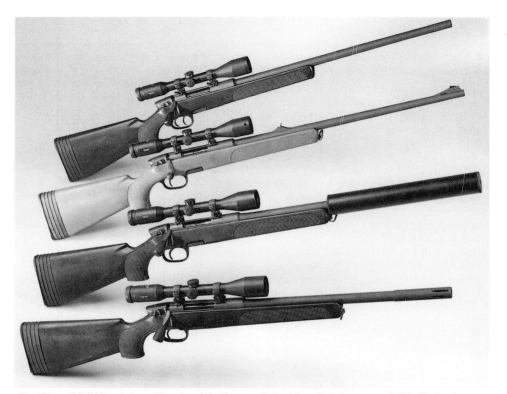

The Steyr SSG69 sniping rifle: (top) Police model with only telescope sight; (below) Standard, with iron and telescope sights; (below) Suppressed model with built-in silencer; (bottom) Special model with short barrel and flash hider.

FN-FAL

Belgium

Manufacturer: Fabrique Nationale d'Armes de Guerre, Herstal

The FN company began developing an automatic rifle in the mid-1930s, and in 1949 produced an excellent traditional design which was adopted by several armies. However, they were astute enough to realise that by adopting modern manufacturing methods and striking away from the traditional wooden-stocked design they could produce a sound weapon at a competitive price. In the early 1950s NATO were wrangling over their standard cartridge and FN gambled that the American proposal which eventually became the 7·62mm round would win. They therefore developed

their new rifle around this cartridge, so that when NATO settled on it, and the members all looked round for a rifle, FN were ready with the **FAL (Fusil Automatique Légère)**. Since 1953, when the first customers appeared, the FAL has been adopted by over 70 armies and has been made under licence in several countries.

The **FAL** is gas operated and uses a tilting bolt mechanism derived from the earlier 1949 rifle. There is a bolt inside a bolt carrier, and the carrier has a shaped cam surface which acts against lugs on each side of the bolt. On firing, gas is directed into a cylinder above the barrel, where it drives a short-stroke piston back to

deliver a sharp blow to the bolt carrier. This starts moving back, and has a short free movement, allowing pressure to drop in the bore, before the cam contacts the bolt lugs and lifts the rear of the bolt up, disengaging it from a locking surface in the receiver. The bolt and carrier then run back and are returned by a spring to reload the chamber. As the bolt closes, the carrier continues forward and another cam surface forces the bolt down into its locking recess. A hammer is cocked during the rearward stroke.

As originally designed the firing mechanism gave single shots and automatic fire, but the rifle is rather light for automatic fire and most

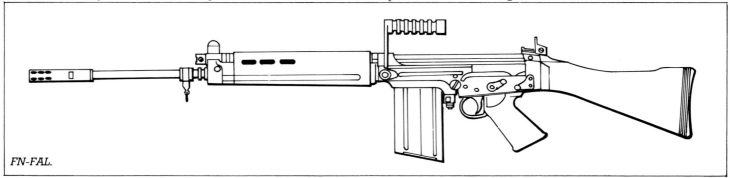

FN-FAL.

customers opted for single shot only mechanisms. A heavy-barrelled version with a bipod was provided for those who wanted a squad automatic weapon.

The standard rifle has a wooden or plastic fixed butt and long barrel. There is also a folding-butt model which can be fitted with the standard long barrel or with a short barrel. A variety of flash eliminators can be found, some of which can be used for grenade launching. In general, the **FN-FAL** could be configured any way the customer wanted it, within limits.

Top: the FN-FAL rifle with short barrel and folding metal butt. Below: with standard barrel and fitted with an image-intensifying night sight.

Specification:
Calibre: 7·62mm NATO
Operation: Gas, semi-automatic or selective fire
Length: 1053mm
Weight: 4·31kg
Barrel: 533mm, 4 grooves, right-hand twist
Magazine: 20-round box
Rate of fire: 650 rds/min.
Muzzle velocity: 853 m/sec.

FN-FNC

Belgium

Manufacturer: FN Herstal SA, Herstal

FN were quick to realise the importance of the 7·62mm NATO cartridge and had a rifle ready for the demand; in the early 1970s they tried to repeat this with a 5·56mm rifle, the CAL, which was more or less a scaled-down FAL model. This, however, appeared at the wrong time, when most armies still had considerable mileage left in their 7·62mm weapons and were not ready to make the change of calibre until everybody else was of the same mind. As a result the CAL rifle failed to find a market; moreover, it was soon found to be too expensive and insufficiently reliable. FN therefore

developed an entirely new 5·56mm assault rifle and entered it into the 1977 NATO trials, but this, too, was premature and the weapon was withdrawn for further development.

In 1982 the new rifle, the **FN-FNC**, eventually appeared. It was a gas-operated weapon but instead of the FAL's tilting bolt or the multiple-thread bolt of the CAL, the **FNC** uses a simple two-lug rotating bolt similar in general principle to that of the M16. A gas piston above the barrel drives back the bolt carrier; inside this is the bolt, the rotation of which is driven by a lug propelled by a cam track in the carrier. A return spring is compressed and the hammer cocked during the recoil

stroke, and the return stroke loads a fresh round into the chamber and rotates the bolt to lock it. The gas regulator is simply an on-off tap, on for normal fire and off for launching grenades. The gas system is self-regulating; whatever amount of gas is required to start the bolt moving is taken, and once the piston moves back it releases any further gas to atmosphere.

Light alloys, pressed steel and plastics are used in the construction, resulting in a commendably light rifle. The firing mechanism offers single shots, three-round bursts or automatic fire. The barrel can be obtained rifled to suit either the original US M193 bullet or

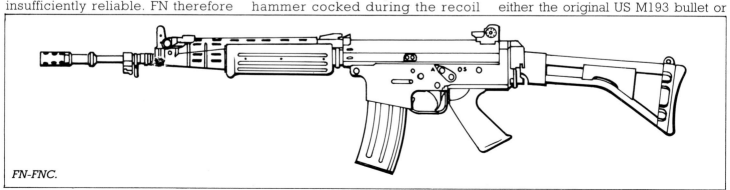

FN-FNC.

the NATO-standardised Belgian SS109 bullet.

The **FNC** is made in two versions; the first is the standard rifle with full length barrel and either a plastic fixed butt or a tubular metal folding butt. The second is a carbine version with a short (363mm) barrel with the same butt options. In addition there is also a **'Law Enforcement'** version of the standard rifle which has a firing mechanism capable only of single shot semi-automatic fire. The **FNC** is in service with the Belgian Army, is made under licence in Indonesia and, in somewhat modified form, is the Swedish Army standard rifle.

The upper picture shows that the FNC is a relatively simple weapon to strip and maintain, while the lower picture shows that it can be used left-handed as well.

Specification (Standard rifle):
Calibre: 5·56mm
Operation: Gas, selective fire
Length (butt extended): 997mm (butt fixed; 766mm (butt folded)
Weight: 3·8kg
Barrel: 449mm, 6 grooves, right-hand twist
Magazine: 30-round box
Rate of fire: 600-750 rds/min.
Muzzle velocity: 965 m/sec.

Manufacturer: Česzkoslovenska Zbrojowka, Uhersky Brod
(Variant Models: 58P, 58V, 58Pi)

The standard rifle of almost all Warsaw Pact and Communist-backed countries was the Kalashnikov AK, with the exception of the armed forces of Czechoslovakia. The Czechs had an extremely good indigenous arms industry by 1939, and they were prompt to get it back into operating order after 1945. As a result they had some excellent weapon designs available, and instead of accepting the Kalashnikov they opted for their own

rifle. The ČZ58 does tend to resemble an AK and fools many people, but it is a totally different weapon.

The weapon is gas operated, with a cylinder mounted above the barrel; there is no gas regulator, the full force of the gas being delivered to the piston, but there are vents in the cylinder which, once the piston has been given sufficient momentum and moved past the vents, allows the surplus gas to escape. The piston makes a short stroke, striking a bolt carrier and driving it rearward. The bolt, inside the carrier, is rectangular

and a hinged locking piece is engaged in front of the shoulders in the receiver. The carrier moves back some 22mm, giving ample time for the chamber pressure to drop, and then inclined planes in the carrier lift the locking piece free from the locking shoulders and then carry the bolt to the rear, extracting the empty case, cocking the hammer and compressing a return spring.

On the return stroke the bolt face collects a cartridge from the magazine and loads it into the chamber. The bolt closes up behind the case, and the

ČZ58.V

carrier, moving forward, drives the locking piece down into the engagement with the shoulders on the receiver, so locking the bolt firmly. On pressing the trigger the hammer strikes a firing pin in the bolt and the cartridge is fired.

The standard model is the **ČZ58P**, with a solid butt; early models used wood but since the early 1960s the butt has been of wood-impregnated plastic material. The **ČZ58V** is the same rifle but with a folding single-strut metal butt which folds sideways to lie alongside the receiver. The **ČZ58Pi** is the standard P model but with a special bracket attached to the right side for mounting a night vision sight. This version usually has a large flash-hider attached to the muzzle and a light bipod.

Specification:

Calibre: 7·62mm Czech M45 or 7·62mm Soviet M43
Operation: Gas, selective fire
Length: 843mm
Weight: 3·11kg
Barrel: 400mm, 4 grooves, right-hand twist
Magazine: 30-round box
Rate of fire: 800 rds/min.
Muzzle velocity: 710 m/sec.

Though it may resemble the Kalashnikov, the Czech service rifle is an entirely different weapon.

SAKO TRG-21 SNIPER'S RIFLE   Finland

Manufacturer: Sako Ltd, Riihimäki

This rifle was introduced in 1989 and represents the most recent thinking in the design of sniping rifles from a company long known for precision weapons.

The **TRG-21** consists of a heavy stainless steel barrel screwed into a tubular receiver. The receiver is, unusually, cold-hammered from steel in the same manner as the barrel, instead of, as is more usual, being machined from the solid. This should give excellent strength for the minimum weight and, due to work-hardening under the hammers, exceptional resistance to wear. The receiver and barrel are attached to an aluminium sub-frame by three screws, so making a completely rigid structure, yet allowing the barrel to float freely. There is a small but efficient muzzle brake at the end of the barrel; it is probable that this can be removed and replaced by a silencer.

The bolt is of conventional type, with three front lugs and a fourth formed by the handle turning down into a recess. The opening movement is a 60° lift.

The trigger mechanism, of high-grade steel, is fully adjustable as to the position of the trigger, so as to suit the firer's hand, and the first-stage travel (first pressure) and weight of pull are also adjustable. A detachable magazine, also of high-grade steel, is concealed inside the stock. There is a silent-operating safety catch on the right side of the receiver, and at the rear of the bolt is an indicator showing whether or not the rifle is cocked.

The stock is made from injection-moulded polyurethane and encloses

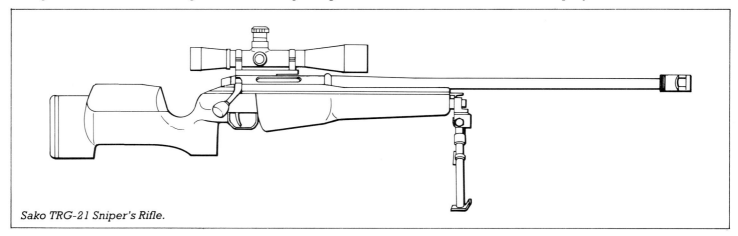

Sako TRG-21 Sniper's Rifle.

the aluminium sub-frame. The butt is formed into a pistol grip and has a series of distance and angle plates provided which allow the user to adjust the length and the height of the cheek-piece to suit his own stature. At the front of the sub-frame an adjustable steel bipod is fitted.

Conventional iron sights are not fitted; there is a 17mm dovetail sight mount formed into the receiver, on to which any preferred optical or electro-optical sight can be fitted. The mount also includes a set of fold-down emergency sights.

As with all sniping rifles the success of this weapon depends largely upon the ammunition, and Sako recommend the use of their own ·308 Winchester special cartridges which are carefully manufactured for precision shooting.

Specification:
Cartridge: 7·62mm NATO (·308 Winchester)
Operation: Manual, single-shot
Length: 1150mm
Weight: 4·7kg without sights
Barrel: 660mm, 4 grooves, right-hand twist
Magazine: 10-round double-row box
Muzzle velocity: 840 m/sec.

The TRG rifles are now available in two calibres; the TRG21 (below) in 7.62mm NATO and the TRG41, similar but chambered for the exceptionally accurate .338 Lapua Magnum cartridge.

FUSIL AUTOMATIQUE MAS (FA-MAS)   France

Manufacturer: Manufacture d'Armes de St Etienne

The French Army was the first European army to adopt the 5·56mm cartridge as their standard infantry calibre, when they introduced the **FA-MAS (Fusil Automatique, Manufacture d'Armes de Saint Etienne)** in 1980. Since then it has been sold to a number of ex-French colonies including Djibuti and Gabon, and to Lebanon and the United Arab Emirates.

The **FA-MAS** is a bullpup rifle, with the action set well back into the stock so as to give maximum barrel length in a compact weapon. The action is delayed blowback, using a two-part bolt of unusual design. The bolt is carried in a heavy bolt carrier and the two are connected by a curved lever; as the bolt closes, the carrier continues forward and rotates the lever forward so that it engages in front of a lug in the floor of the receiver. On firing, the pressure in the chamber forces the

cartridge case back against the bolt; this presses back against the lever and attempts to rotate it backwards so as to lift the toe from the lug. But the top of the lever bears against the heavy bolt carrier, and the leverage ratio means that there is quite a strong resistance to the initial movement. This is sufficient to allow the bullet to leave the barrel and the chamber pressure to drop. Eventually the bolt pressure turns the lever and thrusts the carrier back, lifts the lever toe free and the whole

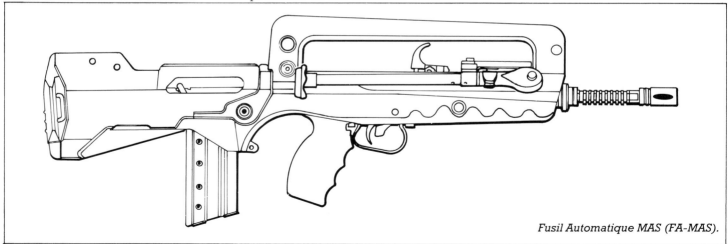

Fusil Automatique MAS (FA-MAS).

104

assembly begins to run backwards to reload and recock the weapon. The locking lever is also interlinked to the firing pin and firing mechanism so that the rifle cannot fire until the lever has rotated into the locked position.

The system works satisfactorily, but is rather marginal – most cartridge cases show signs of bulging, indicating that the bolt has started to move backwards and extract the case before the pressure has reached a really safe figure. As with most blowback weapons using bottle-necked cases, the interior of the chamber is grooved to allow propellant gas to pass down outside the cartridge case and equalise the pressure inside and out, thus preventing the case sticking in the chamber.

Several variant models of the **FA-MAS** have been produced and shown at exhibitions in the past decade, but none have been adopted for military use. These include an export model without automatic fire, a short-barrel '**Commando**' model and a civilian model chambered for the ·222 Remington cartridge and capable only of single shot firing.

Specification:
Calibre: 5·56mm NATO
Operation: Delayed blowback, selective fire with burst firing capability
Length: 757mm
Weight: 3·61kg
Barrel: 488mm, 3 grooves, right-hand twist
Magazine: 25-round box

Rate of fire: 900-1000 rds/min.
Muzzle velocity: 960 m/sec.

The French soldiers call the FA-MAS rifle 'Le Clairon' (the bugle) from the shape of the carrying handle.

SNIPING RIFLE FR-F1 France

Manufacturer: Manufacture d'Armes de St. Etienne (Variant Model: FR-F2)

Traditionally, and like most armies, the French used selected specimens of their standard service rifle as sniping weapons, fitting them with telescope sights. The adoption of the 5·56mm FA-MAS rifle ended this, and it became necessary to develop a specialised sniping rifle. And, also like other armies, the French Army fell back upon its last bolt action weapon, the

MAS Modèle 1936 for the basic mechanism, adapted it into a modern weapon, and called the result the **Fusil à Répétition F1**.

The MAS 36 bolt action uses an unusually large diameter bolt which is in one piece. The two locking lugs are at the rear end and lock into recesses in the side walls of the receiver close to the bridge. The mainspring is inside the hollow firing pin, rather than wrapped around it as is the more usual practice. The bolt handle is turned

down, and differs considerably from the MAS 36 pattern which was bent forward to place it close to the firer's hand to allow rapid fire; this is less necessary on a sniping rifle.

A pistol grip is fitted, and the stock, as with the MAS 36, is in two pieces, fore-end and butt, which are bolted to the deep receiver. A ten-round box magazine is inserted from below, and the bottom of the magazine carries a large rubber pad; when the magazine is removed, this pad can be taken from

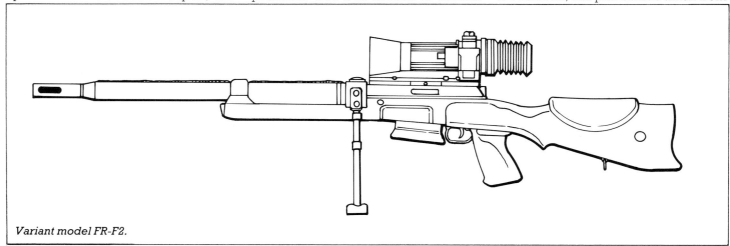

Variant model FR-F2.

the bottom and slipped over the mouth of the magazine to keep out dust and dirt. A bipod is fixed at the rear of the fore-end, and this, together with a muzzle brake, gives the rifle excellent steadiness and a quick return to the aim after firing.

Unlike many sniping rifles, a good set of iron sights, complete with luminous spots for firing in poor light, is fitted, but the primary sight is, of course, a telescope which is issued with the rifle and carried in its own case.

The **FR-F1** was originally issued in 7·5mm French Service calibre, but was later made in 7·62mm NATO chambering.

In 1984 the **FR-F2** rifle was issued; this is much the same but with improvements; the bipod has been strengthened, and slightly moved, to a position where it is less likely to affect barrel vibration, and the fore-end is now of plastic-coated steel. Most novel is the enclosure of the barrel in a thermal insulating sleeve, designed to prevent the barrel bending in strong sunlight, reduce the thermal air disturbance in the sight line and also reduce the infra-red signature of the weapon.

Specification:
Calibre: 7·5mm French or 7·62m NATO
Operation: Manual, single-shot
Weight: 5·20kg
Length: 1138mm
Barrel: 552mm
Magazine: 10-round box
Muzzle velocity: 852 m/sec. (7·62mm)

The FR-F1 (below) and F2 (left) are based upon an elderly bolt action but both are extremely accurate sniping rifles.

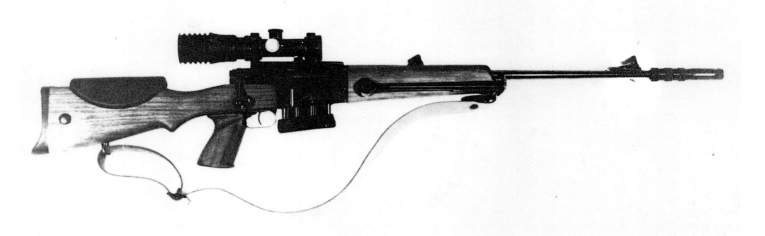

RIFLE G3 Germany

Manufacturer: Heckler & Koch GmbH, Oberndorf-am-Neckar

In 1945 the Mauser factory in Oberndorf was developing a new assault rifle using a roller-locked delayed-blowback breech mechanism. The war ended before the design was perfected, the designers left and settled in Spain, and the rifle development was taken up by CETME. They licensed it to a Dutch company, Nederland Wapen & Munitie, who interested the newly-formed German Army in the design. But the army were not satisfied with it and passed it to

Heckler & Koch to be reworked and brought to perfection. NWM relinquished their licence and Heckler & Koch developed the design into the **Gewehr 3**, which was adopted by the Bundeswehr and has since been widely adopted around the world, being made under licence in several countries. It is probably the most widely-distributed rifle in the Western world after the FN-FAL.

The **G3** breech block is in two pieces; as it closes the heavier rear portion forces out two rollers into recesses in the receiver, so locking the breech. On

firing, the light head is forced back by the cartridge case but has to drive the rollers out of their recesses, in turn forcing the heavy bolt body backwards. This is a slow process, slow enough to allow the bullet to leave the barrel and the bore pressure to drop before the breech begins to open. The bolt then goes back, a hammer is cocked, and in the return stroke the rifle is re-loaded.

The **G3** has one or two innovative features; it was the first to mount the cocking handle well forward on the upper side of the fore-end, so that

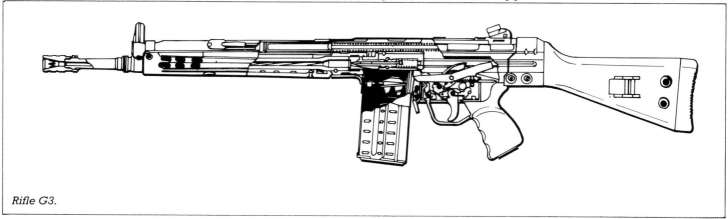

Rifle G3.

108

reaching it is a very easy and natural movement. The bolt has a long, forward, section which runs in the cocking-handle tube and helps to balance the action of the bolt. The chamber has 12 longitudinal grooves cut into its forward surface, so that some of the propellant gas seeps down the outside of the case to balance the internal pressure and so prevent the case sticking too tightly in the chamber, a defect common in blowback-operated weapons.

There are several minor variations; the basic **G3** has a wooden butt and simple two-position rear sight; the **G3A1** has a telescoping butt; the **G3A2** was a **G3** with a drum-type adjustable rear sight which has since become standard on all models; the **G3A3** has a plastic butt and fore-end and is the current model; the **G3A4** has a telescoping stock. The **G3A3ZF** is fitted as standard with a telescope sight, and the **G3/SG1** is a selected **G3A3** with a zoom telescope sight, bipod and precision trigger assembly which is capable of being set to hair-trigger and adjusted for pull-off.

Specification (G3A3):

Calibre: 7·62mm NATO
Length: 1025mm
Weight: 4·40kg
Barrel: 450mm, 4 grooves, right-hand twist
Magazine: 20-round box
Rate of fire: 500-600 rds/min.
Muzzle velocity: 790 m/sec.

Two standard-barrel versions of the G3 rifle, one with collapsible butt and the other with the fixed plastic butt.

RIFLE G41   Germany

Manufacturer: Heckler & Koch GmbH, Oberndorf-am-Neckar

Heckler & Koch followed up the G3 rifle with the HK33, a 5·56mm weapon which appeared in the early 1970s. Like the contemporary FN-CAL it was somewhat ahead of its time, since most major armies were waiting to see what the American experience with 5·56mm was before they committed themselves, but the HK33 made some useful overseas sales and showed that H&K were on the right lines. It was essentially a scaled-down G3 rifle, using exactly the same bolt system and laid out in the same manner.

In the late 1970s the three-round burst idea was becoming popular; at the same time, H&K were working on their caseless G11 rifle, and they doubtless felt that it might be a good idea to develop a new 5·56mm weapon with a three-round burst capability which would be available for export and, if the G11 should fail, might be a fallback for German Army adoption. Whatever the reasoning behind it, the **G41** was developed, and this has proved to be a most impressive rifle.

In essence, once more it is the familiar H&K roller-locked delayed blowback breech system used in the G3 and scaled down to suit the 5·56mm cartridge. The firing mechanism has been redesigned to allow single shots, three-round bursts, or full automatic fire, and the barrel is rifled with a twist of one turn in 178mm so as to suit the new NATO standard 5·56mm bullet. In addition, NATO standardisation has been carried a good deal further; the magazine housing is to NATO

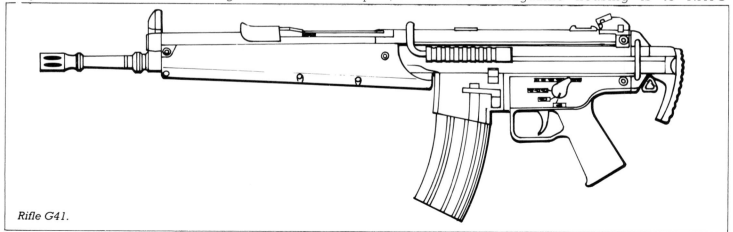

Rifle G41.

Standardisation Agreement (STANAG) 4179 which is based upon the dimensions of the M16 magazine, and thus the **G41** will accept M16 and any other NATO standardised magazine – for example, that of the British L85 rifle. There is also a sight mount to NATO STANAG 2324 which means that any standardised telescope sight or night vision sight will fit on to the **G41**. Other features include a positive bolt closure which is completely silent in operation, a new bolt catch to keep the bolt to the rear after the magazine has been emptied, a mounting for a bipod and a dust cover on the case ejection port.

As with the G3, the **G41** is available with a fixed plastic butt or a telescoping butt, with a long barrel or short barrel. A small number have been purchased by the Bundeswehr; it was originally suggested that when the G11 rifle became standard issue, non-infantry units would be armed with the **G41**, but with the collapse of the G11 it seems unlikely that the **G41** will enter German service in any quantity.

Specification:
Calibre: 5·56mm NATO
Operation: Delayed blowback, selective fire
Length: 997mm (butt fixed); 806mm (butt folded)
Weight: 4·35kg
Barrel: 450mm, 6 grooves, right-hand twist
Magazine: 30-round box
Rate of fire: 850 rds/min.
Muzzle velocity: 935 m/sec.

The H&K G41 rifle with fixed butt. Note the fire selector, giving Safe, Single, Three-round and Automatic positions.

RIFLE G8

Germany

Manufacturer: Heckler & Koch GmbH, Oberndorf-am-Neckar

Following the successful development of their G3 and other rifles, Heckler & Koch applied the same basic delayed-blowback bolt mechanism to a number of light machine gun designs in both 7·62mm and 5·56mm calibres. One of these was the HK11 7·62mm machine gun, which evolved into the HK11E, and this latter design was notable for the fact that it could easily be converted from magazine to belt feed or vice versa. In the early 1980s, in response to various suggestions from European police forces, they redeveloped the HK11E and turned it into the **G8** rifle, a weapon which is one of the most versatile ever manufactured.

The object in view was to develop a weapon which would give a police squad whatever type of firepower they needed to deal with a given situation, without their having to carry a complete armoury around with them. In this one weapon there is every type of response that could possibly be required.

In basic form it is a standard Heckler & Koch delayed blowback rifle, using the familiar roller-locked bolt. It is, though, provided with single shot, three-round burst and automatic fire options, and the barrel is much heavier than usual and precision rifled so that it can act as a perfectly adequate sniping rifle. For this purpose it is fitted not only with standard iron sights but also has a telescope mount which is to NATO standards and will accept any telescope sight or night vision sight.

Where more firepower is required, the standard box magazine can be replaced with a special 50-round drum magazine. Should this not be sufficient,

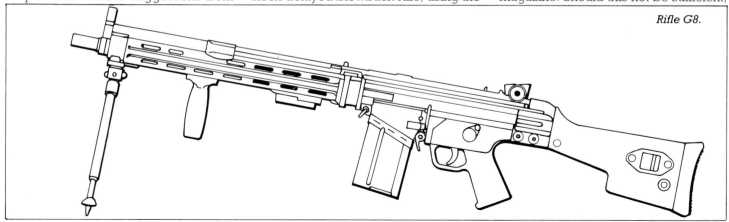

Rifle G8.

then the entire magazine housing can be quickly removed and replaced by a belt feed unit. The bolt is also removed and replaced by a different bolt assembly, and the weapon then becomes a belt-fed machine gun. Since this type of weapon is generally used to produce sustained fire, the barrel of the **G8** can be quickly removed and replaced with a fresh barrel when it gets too hot.

For those forces who do not see a requirement for the automatic fire option, the **G8A1** variant is capable only of single shot fire, but retains the quick-change heavy barrel and telescope sight mounting.

The **G8** has been adopted by the West German Border Police and several other state police forces as armament for their anti-terrorist squads.

Specification:

Calibre: 7·62mm NATO
Operation (G8): Delayed blowback, selective fire
Weight: 8·15kg with bipod
Length: 1030mm
Barrel: 450mm, 6 grooves, right-hand twist
Magazine: 20-round box, 50-round drum or belt
Rate of fire: 800 rds/min.
Muzzle velocity: 835 m/sec.

The G8 rifle is perhaps the most versatile rifle ever made.

RIFLE G11

Germany

Manufacturer: Heckler & Koch GmbH, Oberndorf-am-Neckar

In 1969 the Federal German Army began planning for its next generation of infantry weapons, which would come into service in the 1990s. Their principal demand was for a greatly increased chance of a hit, and designers were given a free hand to develop whatever they thought might achieve this. Three companies sub- mitted proposals, and in 1975 the Heckler & Koch design was selected for further development.

After analysis of the demand, H&K concluded that their only hope lay in a three-round burst at an exceptionally high rate of fire, too high to be reached by a conventional design. This led them to contemplate the use of case- less ammunition, since, among other things, this did away with the extraction and ejection functions and so speeded up reloading. This, in turn, led to problems of breech sealing and high chamber temperatures. A design was produced and submitted to the NATO trials of 1977, but it was premature and suffered from overheating. It was withdrawn and re-worked, and an entirely new propellant was developed which did not react to high chamber temperatures by prematurely firing.

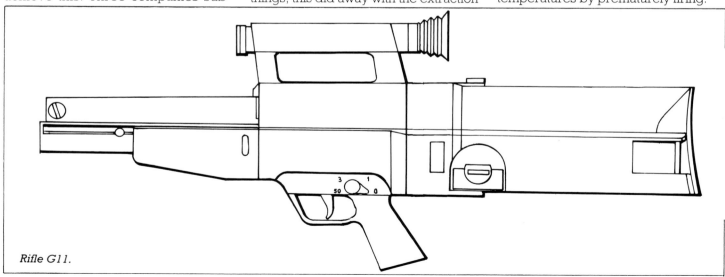

Rifle G11.

The final design consists of a rifle mechanism which floats freely inside an all-enveloping plastic casing. This casing is formed into a carrying handle which also holds a low-power optical sight. The magazine slides into the receiver longitudinally above the barrel and feeds downwards into a rotating breech-block which has the chamber bored in it. Turning the cocking knob feeds a caseless round into the chamber and aligns the chamber with the barrel. Pressing the trigger releases a hammer to fire the cartridge. There is no empty case or residue after firing, and a gas mechanism rotates the breech to collect a fresh round and align it with the barrel. When set for a three-round burst, the mechanism is unique; the first round fires and the internal structure begins to recoil inside the plastic casing. During this movement the second round is chambered and fired, adding to the recoil, and then the third round is chambered and fired, adding even more. Finally, after the third bullet has left the barrel, the recoil stroke is completed and the firer actually feels the kick against his shoulder. Since the three rounds are fired at about 2000 rds/min, they are gone before the rifle can jump, so adding to the accuracy.

The **G11 rifle** underwent extended trials with the German Army and was scheduled to be issued to selected units in 1992. However, the sudden re-unification of East and West Germany led to a slashing of the defence budget in 1990, and among the items dropped was the **G11 rifle**. A limited number have been issued to German Special Forces, but general issue seems unlikely.

Specification:
Calibre: 4·7mm caseless
Operation: Recoil, selective fire
Length: 752·5mm
Weight: 3·80kg
Barrel: 537·5mm, polygonal rifling, right-hand twist
Magazine: 50-round box
Rate of fire: 600 rds/min (automatic); 2000 (burst fire)
Muzzle velocity: 930 m/sec.

The G11 represents a considerable technical advance in small arms design. It was also a contender in the US Army Advanced Combat Rifle trials.

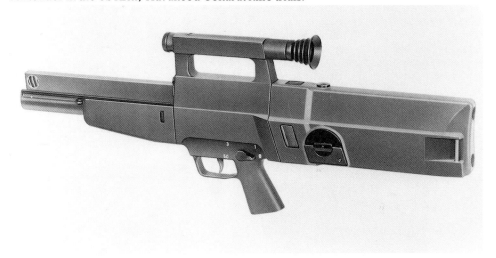

MAUSER SP66   Germany

Manufacturer: Mauser-Werke Oberndorf GmbH, Oberndorf-am-Neckar

The German Army do not tie themselves to one specific weapon in each class, but spread their purchasing around between various makers so as to maintain a sound manufacturing base. As a result, in addition to the Heckler & Koch rifles in the sniping role, they also deploy a large number of **Mauser SP66** rifles.

The **Mauser SP66** is actually based upon a commercial sporting rifle the 'Model SP66S Super Match', though various modifications have been made to suit it to employment by military and police agencies. It is a bolt action rifle using Mauser's 'short action' bolt mechanism; in this design, the bolt handle is actually fitted to the forward end of the bolt, just behind the locking lugs. In point of fact the opening stroke of the bolt is no shorter than any other, since it must move back a finite distance to allow the cartridge to enter the boltway, but the placement of the bolt handle means a much shorter movement of the firer's hand and a quicker return to the trigger after reloading. It does mean that the action body can be some 90mm shorter, and instead of merely using this to shorten the rifle, the saved amount has been added to the barrel length. The barrel is fitted with a very efficient muzzle brake and flash eliminator, specially developed to completely do away with flash, since this rifle is intended to be used with high-power telescope or night vision sights which can easily be blinded by excessive flash.

The wooden stock is of the thumb-hole pattern giving an excellent grip for the firing hand, and the length of butt and height of cheek-piece can be adjusted to suit the firer. All wooden surfaces in contact with the hand have been roughened, the fore-end is wider than usual, and the trigger has a wide shoe so that the hands have a firm grip and control of the weapon.

There are no iron sights fitted; the receiver is formed into a telescope

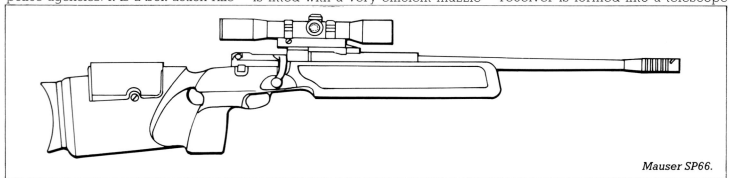

Mauser SP66.

mount and the rifle is supplied as standard with a Zeiss Diavari ZA 1·5x-6x zoom telescope sight. A special adapter to fit on the telescope mount and adapt it to night vision image intensifying sights is also provided.

Two views of the Mauser SP66 fitted with an image-intensifying night sight. It is now available with a specially-fitted silencer in place of the muzzle brake.

Specification:
Calibre: 7·62mm NATO
Operation: Manual, single-shot
Length: Approx. 1200mm depending upon butt adjustment
Weight, empty: 6·12kg with Zeiss telescope
Barrel: 650mm, 6 grooves, right-hand twist
Magazine: 3-round integral box
Muzzle velocity: 868 m/sec.

STURMGEWEHR (StGw.57) 57 Switzerland

Manufacturer: Schweizerische Industrie Gesellschaft, Neuhausen-Rheinfalls

The Schweizerische Industrie Gesellschaft (SIG) have been manufacturing rifles for the Swiss Army since 1869, and in the intervening years they have also developed submachine guns and machine guns, as well as a highly respected line of pistols. They have always had a finger on the pulse of current arms development, and after 1945 they looked closely at many designs which the war had thrown up, among them the Mauser Sturmgewehr 45, a design which was never completed before the war ended. This used an unusual roller-locked breech mechanism, and SIG took this idea and developed it into a practical mechanism, applying it to a rifle which they then offered to the Swiss Army. After trial it was adopted as the **Sturmgewehr 57**, and has remained in use ever since; most first-line Swiss units are now re-equipping with the 5·56mm StGw.90, but reservists and second-line formations still use the **StGw.57**.

The most immediately obvious feature of the **StGw.57** is the 'straight-line' layout, the axis of the barrel and the top of the butt lying in a perfectly straight line. This means that the recoil force passes straight down the weapon and into the shoulder; weapons with conventionally sloped butts drive the recoil force back some inches above the point of contact with the shoulder and thus the rifle tends to lift the muzzle at each shot. The **StGw.57** is remarkably steady and very accurate.

The bolt mechanism is in two parts, a light head and a heavy body, with two rollers separating the units. As the bolt closes the nose of the body forces the rollers out and locks them into recesses in the receiver. On firing, the bolt head tends to set back, but it cannot open due to the rollers; pressure on the rollers is transmitted to the

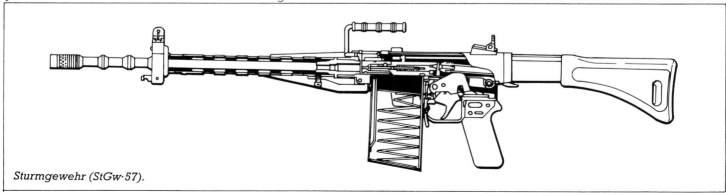

Sturmgewehr (StGw·57).

bolt body, and is assisted by a controlled leak of gas around the cartridge and through holes in the bolt head, which impinges on the bolt body. These two forces combine to move the bolt body back, so leaving room for the rollers to be forced inwards by the bolt head, and eventually the rollers come free from the recesses and the bolt opens.

The **StGw.57** is provided with a folding bipod, and it is also possible to launch grenades from the muzzle.

Although somewhat heavy by today's standards, the StuG57 is an accurate and reliable weapon which has armed the Swiss for the past 35 years. It will remain in use as a reserve weapon for many more years, even though service calibre has now been changed to 5.56mm.

Specification:
Calibre: 7·5mm Swiss
Operation: Delayed blowback, selective fire
Length: 1105mm
Weight: 5·55kg
Barrel: 583mm, 4 grooves, right-hand twist
Magazine: 24-round box
Rate of fire: 450-500 rds/min.
Muzzle velocity: 760 m/sec.

GALIL RIFLE   Israel

Manufacturer: Ta'as Israel Industries, Ramat Hasharon

The Israeli Defence Force adopted the 7·62mm FN-FAL in the early 1950s, but experience in their various wars with Arab nations convinced them that something lighter and more handy was necessary. After the 1967 Arab-Israeli war, the IDF asked for a new rifle, and the **Galil** was the result, appearing in 1973.

The designer spent some time in studying and testing every available rifle, and soon came to the conclusion that the reliability of the Soviet AK rifle, which was in extensive Arab use, was of vital importance in a desert environment. He therefore took the AK as his model but then designed out various points which were generally thought to be defects and added a few things which combat experience had suggested might be worthwhile. The calibre of 5·56mm was selected, though in later years, and principally for export sales, the rifle has also been made in 7·62mm calibre.

The AK is generally thought to have two prime defects; it is inaccurate and the fire selection lever is clumsy and noisy in operation. The **Galil** cured both these; by adopting 5·56mm but generally retaining the bulk of the AK, the result was rather heavy for the calibre which gave the weapon strength and also resisted the recoil force and thus improved accuracy. The fire selector was changed into a small thumb-operated switch above

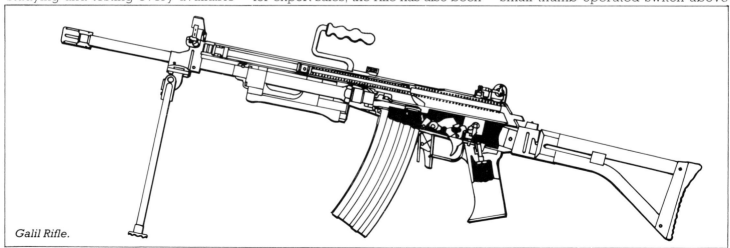

Galil Rifle.

the pistol grip on both sides of the rifle so that it is easily operated by right- or left-handed shooters. The operating system is the same top-mounted gas piston, bolt carrier and rotating bolt, and the hammer firing mechanism is also broadly similar to that of the AK. A bipod is fitted, which also acts as a wire-cutter and a bottle-opener, two examples of combat-oriented additions due to practical experience. The sights are provided with fold-up auxiliary leaves which carry luminous spots for firing in poor light, and they are generally agreed to be probably the best of their kind.

The standard rifle is known as the **ARM** and has a bipod, carrying handle and folding butt. The **Model AR** is similar but does not have the bipod or carrying handle. The **Model SAR** has a shorter (332mm) barrel, folding butt, no bipod and no carrying handle.

The **Galil** has been sold to other countries, and has also been copied in slightly modified form by the South African Defence Force who adopted it as the **R-4 rifle**, later developing a short-barrelled carbine version known as the **R-5**.

Specification (Model ARM):
Calibre: 5·56mm
Operation: Gas, selective fire
Length: 979mm (butt fixed),
742mm (butt folded)
Weight: 4·35kg
Barrel: 460mm, 6 grooves, right-hand twist
Magazine: 35-round box

Rate of fire: 650 rds/min.
Muzzle velocity: 950 m/sec.

The Galil has elements of Kalashnikov's design in it, but is far more versatile, capable of launching grenades or functioning as the squad light machine gun when fitted with an extra-capacity magazine.

GALIL SNIPER'S RIFLE   Israel

Manufacturer: Ta'as Israel Industries, Ramat Hasharon

As noted above, in discussing the 5·56mm Galil assault rifle, the design was also made somewhat larger in 7·62mm, principally for export. In the late 1970s, however, the Israel Defence Force expressed a requirement for a new sniping rifle to replace the elderly Mauser bolt-action weapons they were using in this role, and asked Israel Military Industries, makers of the Galil, to develop a suitable weapon. They took the 7·62mm Galil as their starting point

and, in close co-operation with the IDF, turned it into a highly specialised sniping weapon.

The basic mechanism is the same Kalashnikov-derived rotating bolt, operated by a gas piston and bolt carrier, as is used in the smaller Galil, merely enlarged and strengthened to deal with the heavier cartridge. The barrel is much heavier than would be used on an ordinary service rifle, giving stiffness and exceptional accuracy. The fore-end is fitted so that it does not interfere with the natural vibration of the barrel, and the

adjustable bipod is assembled to the fore-end so as not to place any strain on the rifle itself. Moreover, the bipod is set well back so that it is possible for the sniper to reach out and adjust it without having to expose himself or shift the rifle.

The muzzle is threaded and fitted with a very efficient muzzle brake and flash eliminator which assists concealment and prevents the rifle moving too far from the aim on firing. It can be unscrewed and replaced with a silencer if required.

There is, of course, no automatic fire

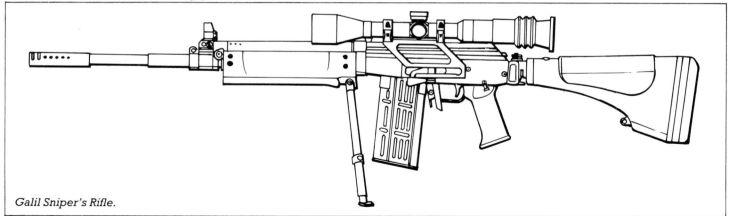

Galil Sniper's Rifle.

option; the trigger is a carefully assembled two-stage mechanism giving a graduated pull and crisp release. The butt folds for ease of carriage, and locks very rigidly when in the firing position. It carries a cheek-piece which is adjustable for height, and spacers can be placed beneath the rubber recoil pad to adjust for length.

There is a very rigid telescope mount assembled to the left side of the receiver by a quick-release system. The 6x40 telescope fits to this mount, and the telescope and mount can be quickly removed from the rifle and replaced without disturbing the zero point.

Each rifle is supplied in a specially-designed transit case which also carries the telescope and mount, optical filters for the telescope, firing and carrying slings, spare magazines and cleaning equipment. Using 7·62mm Match Grade ammunition, the Galil Sniper can easily place all its shots inside a 12cm circle at 300 metres range.

Specification:
Calibre: 7·62mm NATO
Operation: Gas, semi-automatic
Length: 1115mm (butt fixed);
840mm (butt folded)
Weight: 6·4kg

Barrel: 508mm without muzzle brake; 4 grooves, right-hand twist
Magazine: 20-round box
Muzzle velocity: 815 m/sec.

The Sniper is a selected Galil rifle in 7.62mm with special sights and other fittings.

BERETTA 70/90   # Italy

Manufacturer: Pietro Beretta SpA, Gardone Val Trompia

In the early 1980s the Italian Army decided that it would replace the 7·62mm with 5·56mm weapons and issued a fairly broad specification, inviting manufacturers to submit designs. By this time Beretta had some field experience with their AR70/223 rifle and had found some minor deficiencies in the design, so they set about rectifying these to produce a suitable weapon for submission.

The receiver of the AR70/223 was a pressed steel box with the bolt guides pressed in, and in severe circumstances it had been found to distort sufficiently to jam the bolt. The receiver was therefore re-designed in a stronger form with welded-on bolt guide rails. The firing mechanism is designed to produce single shots, three-round bursts or automatic fire, and is so designed that it can be pre-set to give any two of these options. The weapon is gas operated, using a bolt carrier and rotating bolt driven by a gas piston. There is a carrying handle which can be easily removed to expose a telescope sight mount; the carrying handle mounting is pierced to give a through line of sight for the standard iron sights.

One of the most innovative things about this weapon is that the barrel is carefully manufactured with a collar which butts on to the receiver and so locates the chamber in the correct position in relation to the bolt, so that no adjustment for headspace is required when replacing a barrel. The barrel is retained in place by a threaded nut which clamps the collar tightly to the receiver face.

In addition to the standard rifle there is a carbine version, the **SC70/90**, which differs only in having a folding metal butt-stock. There is also a Special Service Carbine, **SCS70/90** which has the same folding butt-stock and also a shorter barrel. The rifle and carbine have their muzzle shaped for grenade launching and are capable of shutting off the gas regulator when firing

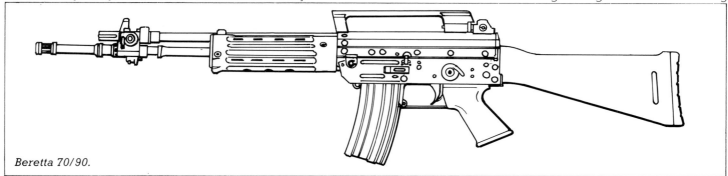

Beretta 70/90.

grenades. There is also a heavy-barrelled version of the rifle which is intended for use as the squad light automatic.

The rifle was submitted for trial in 1985, together with three other designs from different manufacturers. In June 1990 it was approved for adoption by the Italian armed forces.

Beretta incorporated lessons from earlier designs into the AR70/90. Top: the standard length rifle with fixed butt. Below: the carbine version with butt folded.

Specification (AR70/90):
Calibre: 5·56mm NATO
Operation: Gas, selective fire
Length: 998mm
Weight: 3·99kg
Barrel: 450mm, 6 grooves, right-hand twist
Magazine: 30-round box
Rate of fire: 600 rds/min. (estimated)
Muzzle velocity: 900 m/sec.

BERETTA AR70/·223   Italy

Manufacturer: Pietro Beretta SpA, Gardone Val Trompia

In the 1970s the 5·56mm cartridge began to assume an important place in the world's armouries, and the Pietro Beretta company considered it was time that they offered a rifle in this calibre; they were also alert to the fact that by that time the 7·62mm BM59 rifle was becoming obsolete and that there was a strong movement towards re-arming in 5·56mm calibre.

The **Beretta AR70/·223** rifle was a light, gas-operated weapon using a rotating bolt and capable of delivering either single shots or full-automatic fire. Lke most other 5·56mm rifles of the time it made extensive use of steel pressings and welding, and the butt, pistol grip and fore-end were of plastic material. The principal structure was welded, and component parts were attached by spring catches and removeable pins. The muzzle was formed into a combination of flash hider and grenade launcher, and a special folding front sight was fitted for aiming grenades. This sight was connected to the gas regulator; when lifted to take aim, the sight automatically cut off the supply of gas to the piston, so that the breech did not open and all the gas generated by the special grenade-launching cartridge was delivered to the base of the grenade toobtain the maximum range.

The **AR70/·223** was the standard rifle with a 450mm barrel. A version for mechanised troops was the **SC70**, similar in general design but with a folding metal butt-stock. A third version, designed for use by airborne or commando troops requiring a more compact weapon, was the SC70 Short, which had a 320mm barrel with the same folding butt-stock.

Although tested by the Italian Army the AR70 family was not generally

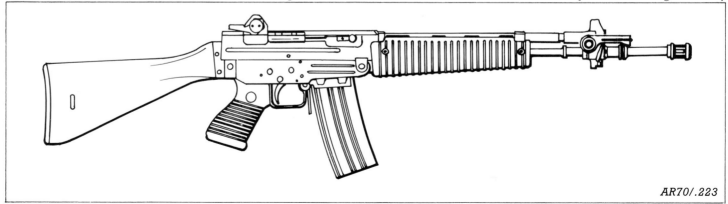

AR70/.223

adopted, though numbers were taken into use by Italian Special Forces units. It was then sold to Jordan and Malaysia and some other countries.

Top: The SC70/.223 with first-pattern butt. Below: The AR70/.223 was Beretta's first venture into the 5.56mm assault rifle field, and though adopted in small numbers, it was too early for the Italian Army: but it gave Beretta the chance to learn useful lessons before they designed the 70/90 model.

Specification:
Calibre: 5·56mm M193
Operation: Gas, selective fire
Length: 955mm
Weight: 3·50kg
Barrel: 450mm, 4 grooves, right-hand twist
Magazine: 30-round box
Rate of fire: 650 rds/min.
Muzzle velocity: 950 m/sec.

BERETTA SNIPER

Italy

Manufacturer: Pietro Beretta SpA, Gardone Val Trompia

This is a conventional bolt-action magazine rifle, using a modified form of Mauser bolt with front locking lugs. The heavy barrel is free-floating in the stock and is fitted with a flash hider. A tube beneath the barrel, mostly concealed within the stock, is attached to the receiver and contains an harmonic balancer, a weight and springs which tend to remain in the same spatial position during recoil and thus damp out the vibrations of the barrel which produce inaccurate and inconsistent shooting. The end of this tube is also used to mount the folding bipod, and it also carries a sliding hand-stop which can be used as a forward attachment point for a sling.

The high quality wooden stock has a thumb-hole, for a comfortable grip, and is fitted with a cheek-piece which can be adjusted for height so that the firer's face always takes up the same position relative to the sights. There is a rubber recoil pad on the end of the butt which is capable of being removed, and between it and the butt spacers can be inserted so as to fit the length of the butt to the firer's reach.

The standard sights are of target-shooting quality; the front sight is a blade protected by a hood which also prevents reflections from the blade. The rear sight is a V-notch which is capable of adjustment for elevation and windage. As a sniping rifle, though, it is to be expected that a telescope sight will be used and the receiver has dovetail sight mounts in front of and behind the loading aperture. The manufacturers recommend, and fit as standard, the Zeiss Diavari-Z telescope, which has

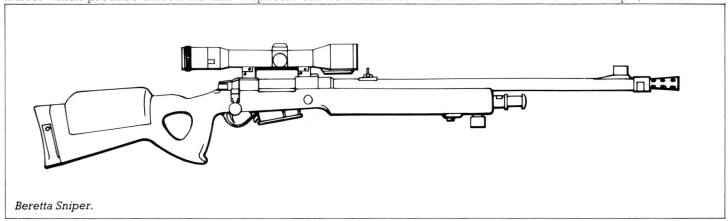

Beretta Sniper.

variable zoom magnification from 1·5x to 6x and can be provided with a variety of graticules matched to the ammunition. The sight mount is to the NATO STANAG 2324 and thus when the telescope is removed any NATO-standard night vision sight or other optical sight can be fitted in its place. The Beretta Sniper has been adopted by a number of European police forces and by armies in other parts of the world.

Specification:
Calibre: 7·62mm NATO
Operation: Manual, single-shot
Length: 1165mm
Weight: 5·55kg empty without sights or bipod
Barrel: 586mm, 4 grooves, right-hand twist
Magazine: 5-round box
Muzzle velocity: 845m/sec.

Like many other armies, the Italians prefer a bolt-action rifle for their sniping weapon, and the Beretta also uses a traditional wooden stock instead of the fashionable plastic.

Manufacturer: Våpensmia A/S, Dokka

The Norwegians, like the Swiss, have always had a high regard for individual marksmanship, and a good sniping rifle has always been an important part of the Norwegian Army's inventory. They retained the Krag-Jørgensen rifle as a sniper until after 1945, many years after every other user of the Krag had scrapped it, and after that they adopted Mausers. In 1988 they adopted the **NM149S**, manufactured by a small company specialising in target weapons and shooting equipment.

The **NM149S** uses a modified Mauser Model 1898 bolt action, generally conceded to be the most secure and precise bolt action ever made. This is allied to a cold-forged heavy barrel, and the entire unit is bedded into a stock fabricated from 28 layers of beech veneer which is chemically impregnated with resin to give strength and make the wood entirely proof against moisture and warping in service. There are two designs of stock; the military version is the more slender of the two, and the police version, in addition to being deeper, is provided with a cheek-piece which

can be adjusted for height. Both types of stock have a synthetic butt-plate, and the length of the butt can be adjusted by removing the butt-plate and adding one or two spacer blocks.

The trigger is of target match specification and is adjustable for pull. the magazine is a five-shot box which is removed from the bottom of the rifle for reloading, since the low-set sights prevent loading from the top of the action.

The rifle is fitted with two sets of sights. The primary sight is a telescope which mounts on to a steel bar running across the top of the receiver above the

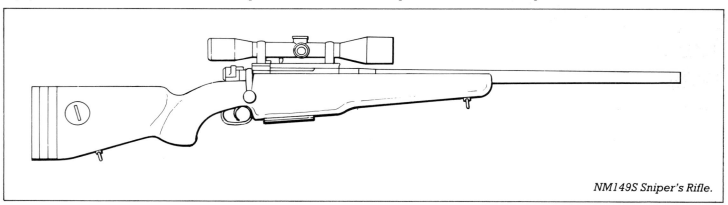

NM149S Sniper's Rifle.

boltway; in this position, although it prevents loading the magazine, it does not interfere with ejection of the fired case. The standard telescope is a Schmidt & Bender 6x42 which is adjustable for ranges from 100 to 800 metres. Alternatively, a 4x36 or a 6x42 zoom telescope can be supplied. The telescope fits on to the mount bar with a quick-release which allows instant removal and replacement without affecting zero. The secondary sight is an adjustable aperture rear sight attached to the sight mount bar, and a blade foresight, both of which can be adjusted for zero to any desired range.

Specification:
Calibre: 7·62mm NATO
Operation: Manual, single-shot
Length: 1120mm
Weight, empty: 5·6kg with telescope
Barrel: 600mm, 4 grooves, right-hand twist
Magazine: 5-shot detachable box
Muzzle velocity: 838 m/sec.

By using a very heavy and stiff barrel, allied to a thoroughly reliable bolt action, the NM149S produces exceptional accuracy out to long ranges and withstands climatic extremes.

SR88 ASSAULT RIFLE Singapore

Manufacturer: Chartered Firearms Industries Pte Ltd

The **SR88** is an improved version of the SAR80 in most respects. The lower receiver is an aluminium forging, reducing the weight without impairing the rigidity of the assembly, and the bolt carrier and bolt use a similar double-rod support system to that used on the earlier rifle. The gas cylinder is above the barrel, and it, the piston and the gas regulator are all chromium-plated to reduce wear and prevent the build-up of gas fouling during prolonged firing. The upper receiver is a steel pressing, and the barrel is cold-forged steel with a chromium-plated chamber. The barrel is fitted with a flash suppressor which vents sideways and upwards, and is internally threaded to accept a blank-firing attachment. The barrel is attached to the receiver by a key and locknut, a system which simplifies assembly and allows for rapid field replacement of a damaged barrel without the need for long adjustment of the cartridge headspace. The hand-guard has been designed so that the US M203 grenade launcher can easily be fitted to the rifle without modification.

The firing pin is provided with a spring which keeps the pin to the rear of the bolt except when struck by the firing hammer. This feature is a safety device which prevents the firing pin being flung forward and firing a sensitive cap if the rifle is accidentally dropped or struck. The firing mechanism provides for single shots and either automatic fire or three-round bursts, according to the purchaser's wishes. The cocking handle has an automatic lock to provide for positive and silent bolt closing.

The fixed butt is of glass-reinforced nylon. There is also a version in which the butt is formed of two lightweight tubes, hinged to the rear of the receiver so that it can fold sideways

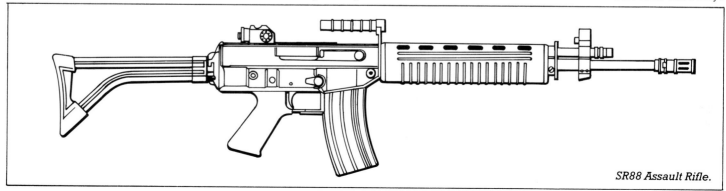

SR88 Assault Rifle.

132

and lie alongside the receiver. The length of either type of butt can be adjusted by removing the butt-plate and pad and inserting spacers.

A carbine version, with a shorter barrel, is also available in fixed or folding butt configuration. All versions are fitted with a fully adjustable rear sight, and both rear and front sights have luminous spots for aiming assistance in poor light. In addition, the upper receiver is formed into a dovetail for mounting any type of optical sight or night vision sight.

Singapore began rifle production by building the M16 under license; the SR88 adopted a similar bolt mechanism but the remainder is of their own design. Here are the standard and carbine versions, both with tubular folding butt.

Specification:
Calibre: 5·56mm NATO
Operation: Gas, selective fire
Length: 970mm
Weight: 3·66kg
Barrel: 459mm, 6 grooves, right-hand twist
Magazine: 20- or 30-round box
Rate of fire: 750 rds/min.
Muzzle velocity: 970 m/sec.

KALASHNIKOV AK-74   Former Soviet Union

Manufacturer: State Arsenals
(Variant Model: AKS-74)

In the 1960s the US Army adopted the 5·56mm calibre and led the subsequent move into the so-called 'micro-calibre' era. There was speculation at the time as to whether the Soviets would follow this lead, since it was known that a ·22 calibre version of the **AK47** had been developed for sport shooting and that the Soviets had a long history of experiments with small-calibre, short-case cartridges. However, it was not until 1979 that rumours began to reach the west of a small-calibre Soviet rifle, and it was first seen in a parade in Moscow in 1980, carried by Paratroops.

This new weapon was soon identified as the **AK-74**; as with previous Kalashnikov models, the standard rifle had a wooden butt, while the **AKS-74** version – which is, in fact, more common than the **AK-74** – has a folding metal butt. This is of an entirely new design, folding sideways to lie alongside the receiver, instead of folding underneath as did previous models.

The calibre selected is 5·45mm; as with most Soviet cartridges, suffici-ently close to a Western calibre to give comparable effects but of different dimensions so that Soviet ammunition cannot be used in Western rifles. The performance is slightly lower than might be expected but comparable with the 5·56mm cartridge in most respects. The rifle mechanism and general construction is exactly the same as the **AK47/AKM** series, so much so that it has been suggested that early models were re-barrelled AKM rifles. The principal exterior difference is the adoption of a complex muzzle brake and compensator

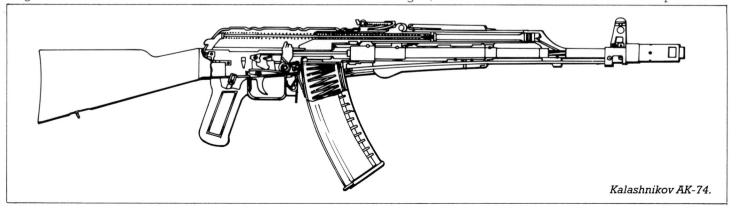

Kalashnikov AK-74.

which directs gas upwards and sideways to reduce recoil and muzzle lift when firing automatic. The drawback to this is that a high proportion of gas is directed sideways, to the discomfort of the firer's companions, but it certainly allows the rifle to have a very low recoil and be very controllable in automatic fire. It is, though, noticeable that this device does nothing to reduce muzzle flash.

Although originally issued to parachute and other specialist troops, by the mid-1980s the **AK-74** had become the standard Soviet Army rifle and had replaced the AKM. It was later put into production in other Warsaw Pact countries, and China, Romania and Bulgaria have also developed versions chambered for the Western 5·56mm cartridge, presumably for export sales.

Specification:
Calibre: 5·45mm Soviet
Operation: Gas, selective fire
Length: 930mm
Weight: 3·60kg
Barrel: 400mm, 4 grooves, right-hand twist
Magazine: 30-round box
Rate of fire: 650 rds/min.
Muzzle velocity: 900 m/sec.

The AK74 is simply the basic AK47 re-designed so as to fire a reduced calibre 5.45mm cartridge, a move which followed the US adoption of the 5.56mm cartridge. Note the adoption of a muzzle brake to improve accuracy in automatic fire.

KALASHNIKOV AK47   Former Soviet Union

Manufacturer: State Arsenals
(Variant Models: AKS47, AKM,
AKMS)

The **Kalashnikov AK47** assault rifle appeared in 1947 and was originally conceived as a replacement for the wartime submachine guns, the Simonov SKS being seen as the standard infantry rifle. However, its virtues of simplicity, reliability and cheapness, together with its adequate short-range performance, soon led to it supplanting the SKS and becoming the standard Soviet, and later Warsaw Pact, service rifle. It was supplied in prodigious quantities to fellow-travelling countries, to nationalist and

other guerillas, and it has been estimated that some 20-30 million have been made, in Russia and other countries. It is certainly the most widely-distributed rifle in history.

The mechanism is gas operated, with a rotating bolt, and is somewhat unusual in having the gas piston attached to the bolt carrier. There is a hammer mechanism which is cocked by the recoiling bolt, and a selector lever on the right side acts as a safety catch and selects single shots or automatic fire. It also blocks the cocking handle travel when in the safe position, though the bolt can be drawn back enough to see whether the chamber is loaded.

The standard **AK47** used a fixed wooden butt, and it was soon followed by the **AKS47** which had a folding metal butt which appears to have been copied from the German MP38 sub-machine gun. Both models were made in the traditional fashion, the receiver being machined from solid steel. This made for a strong weapon but was slow and expensive to manufacture, and the design was therefore changed, adopting a receiver made from pressed and welded steel. This model was known as the **AKM** – M for 'modernised' – and appeared in 1959. The bolt locking system was also simplified, the bolt locking into a

Kalashnikov AK47.

sleeve attached to the rear of the barrel instead of into the actual chamber. Other improvements and changes included removing the holes from the gas cylinder, replacing them with pressed grooves, and pressing two indentations into the receiver body to act as guides for the magazine. As with the **AK47**, the standard **AKM** has a wooden butt, while the **AKMS** has a folding steel butt.

Various members of the Warsaw Pact and other countries have developed their own versions of the **AK** which, while retaining the same basic features, add something which they consider necessary; thus the Romanian and Hungarian versions have forward vertical pistol grips, the Poles have a long grenade launcher muzzle and so forth.

Specification (AKM):
Calibre: 7·62mm Soviet M43
Operation: Gas, selective fire
Length: 876mm
Weight: 3·15kg
Barrel: 414mm, 4 grooves, right-hand twist
Magazine: 30-round box
Rate of fire: 600 rds/min.
Muzzle velocity: 715 m/sec.

Perhaps the most widely-distributed and most-manufactured rifle in history, the Kalashnikov comes in various versions; (top) the standard AKM model with fixed wooden butt, and (below) the AKMS with folding metal butt.

SIMONOV CARBINE (SKS)   Former Soviet Union

Manufacturer: State Arsenals

Sergei Simonov was a skilled Soviet weapon designer who, as early as 1936, had provided the Red Army with an automatic rifle and followed it with an anti-tank rifle in 1941. By this time the Soviets were experimenting with short cartridges, though they dropped the idea for some time after the German invasion. Then, in 1943, the German 7·92mm Short cartridge was deployed against them and they went back to their project and developed the 7·62x39mm M1943 cartridge. Simonov was given the task of providing a suitable automatic rifle to fire it.

The **Simonov SKS** rifle did not appear until after the war, and within ten years was superseded by the Kalashnikov weapons, but it was retained as a ceremonial rifle, in reserve, and was manufactured by several Communist countries including East Germany, China, North Korea and Yugoslavia for many years. It is a simple and robust weapon, easy to operate and maintain, which is probably the reason for its long life.

The breech closure system was adapted by Simonov from his wartime anti-tank rifle design. The bolt is rectangular in section and is held inside a bolt carrier; the carrier has shaped ramps which control the movement of the bolt. Above the barrel is a gas cylinder containing a piston and rod; on firing, gas is vented into the cylinder to drive the piston rod back. It strikes the front of the bolt carrier and starts it moving backwards. The ramps in the carrier lift the rear end of the bolt clear from a recess in the floor of the receiver, and then the bolt is carried back against the pressure of a spring, extracting the fired case. The return spring then drives the carrier back, the bolt strips a round from the magazine and pushes

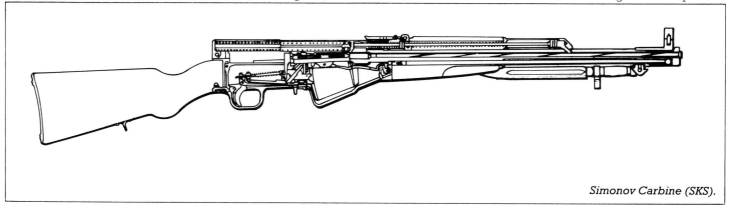

Simonov Carbine (SKS).

it into the chamber. As the bolt stops, tight against the cartridge, the carrier continues to move forward for a short distance and the ramps now force the rear end back down into the locking recess. A hammer fires the cartridge by means of a firing pin in the bolt.

The magazine is inside the stock and is loaded by a charger through the open action; it can be hinged open from below to unload without having to cycle the bolt mechanism. As with most Soviet weapons of the time, the Simonov was given a permanently-attached bayonet which hinges back and lies in a slot in the fore-end.

Specification:
Calibre: 7·62mm M43
Operation: Gas, semi-automatic
Length: 1022mm
Weight: 3·86kg
Barrel: 520mm, 4 grooves, right-hand twist
Magazine: 10-round integral box
Muzzle velocity: 735 m/sec.

The Simonov was the first Soviet rifle to use the M1943 short 7.62mm cartridge, but it was soon superseded by the AK47. Nevertheless, it was widely exported and copied in several Communist countries.

CETME MODELS L and LC

Spain

Manufacturer: Empresa Nacional 'Santa Barbara', Madrid

In the aftermath of World War II several German weapon designers and technicians made their way to Spain, taking with them their knowledge of many wartime German development programmes. Some went to work for a Spanish government arms development 'think-tank' called CETME (Company for Technical Studies of Special Materials), and when CETME were called upon to develop a modern rifle for the Spanish Army,

they resurrected a Mauser design for an assault rifle known as the Sturmgewehr 45 which had been brought to a halt by the end of the war. The important feature of this rifle was its bolt design. The rifle was a delayed blowback weapon, intended for the short 7·92mm cartridge, and adopted a two-piece bolt separated by two rollers. As the bolt closed, the heavy rear section forced the rollers outwards into recesses in the receiver. When the rifle was fired, the pressure forced the cartridge back and pushed

the light bolt head against the rollers, trying to force them out of the recesses. To move, the rollers had, in turn, to push back the bolt body at a considerable mechanical disadvantage. They eventually perfected this design, which was later adopted by Heckler & Koch for their series of rifles. The CETME Model A was the first rifle to appear, but this had technical drawbacks and was succeeded by the Models B and C, the latter being adopted in 7·62mm calibre as the Spanish Army rifle. When, in the late

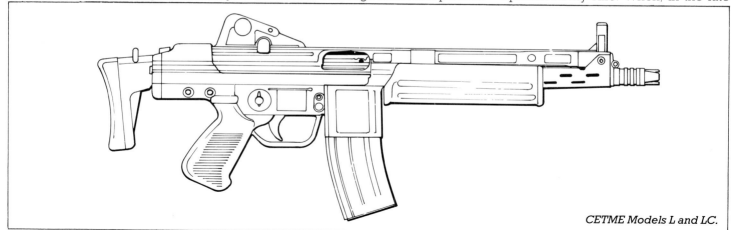

CETME Models L and LC.

140

1970s, the Spanish Army decided to go to 5·56mm, the design was overhauled and the result was the **CETME Model L**.

The **Model L** is a modern assault rifle, with a pressed-steel receiver and plastic furniture. The bolt mechanism is the same roller-locked delayed blowback pioneered in the Model A, though slightly improved in minor details over the years. First models had a three-round burst facility and used a 20-round magazine, but these weapons were soon dropped and the service version has the option of single shots or automatic fire and uses the M16 type of magazine interface. The **Model L** is a fixed-butt weapon, standard for most of the Army. The **Model LC** is a short-barrelled (320mm) version with a butt formed from two metal arms which telescope in alongside the receiver for compactness, and is used by airborne and some mechanised troops. Both models began entering Spanish Army service in 1988.

Specification (Model L):
Calibre: 5·56mm NATO
Operation: Delayed blowback, selective fire
Length: 925mm
Weight: 3·40kg
Barrel: 400mm, 6 grooves, right-hand twist
Magazine: 30-round box
Rate of fire: 700 rds/min.
Muzzle velocity: 875 m/sec.

A member of the Spanish Special Forces using a CETME Model L rifle fitted with telescope sight. The drawing (left) shows the Model LC carbine with collapsible butt.

SG510 ASSAULT RIFLE Switzerland

Manufacturer: Schweizerische Industrie Gesellschaft, Neuhausen-Rheinfalls

In the early 1950s the SIG company developed their AM55 assault rifle, which was adopted by the Swiss Army as the Stgw 57, and is described elsewhere. At that time the 7·62x51mm cartridge had just been standardised by NATO and SIG felt that the same rifle converted to fire the 7·62mm cartridge might well be a commercial success. The result was the **SIG SG510** series, which might therefore be

considered as the commercial equivalent of the Stgw 57.

The same system of delayed blowback action is employed; the chamber is fluted, in order to even the gas pressure on both sides of the cartridge case and so ease extraction, and two of the flutes are extended back to the chamber face, where they lie opposite two small holes in the face of the bolt head. On firing, the bolt head tries to move back, propelled by the pressure in the cartridge case, but is restrained by the presence of two rollers behind

it, which are wedged into recesses in the receiver. The pressure of the bolt head on these rollers is transferred to the bolt body; pressure is also applied by gas passing down the two extended flutes and through the holes in the bolt head, to impinge directly on to the front of the bolt body. These two forces combine to push the bolt body back far enough to allow the rollers to come free from their recesses. As soon as this happens, the impulse on the bolt head drives both head and body backwards against the pressure of a

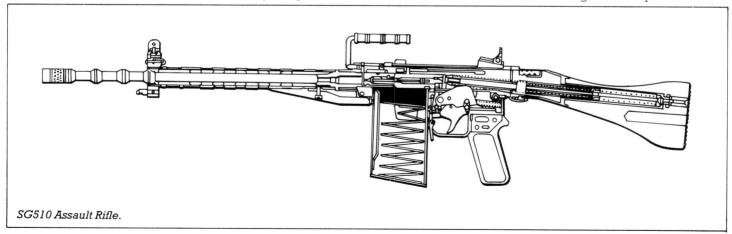

SG510 Assault Rifle.

return spring. When the bolt comes forward it strips a round from the magazine and chambers it, after which the bolt head stops and the bolt body, moving forward, forces the rollers back into their recesses.

There were a number of versions of the **SIG 510**. The basic **510-1** was more or less the Stgw 57 but translated into 7·62 NATO calibre. The **510-2** was similar but used light alloy in many components in order to reduce the weight, though this also increased the recoil. The **510-3** was the first Western rifle to be chambered for the 7·62x39mm Soviet M43 cartridge, in an endeavour to attract business from countries using Soviet weapons; and the **510-4** was an improved model of the **510-1** with a wooden butt and fore-end. Although the **510** was probably the best selective-fire rifle ever made, it was expensive and attracted few sales. Only the armies of Bolivia and Chile adopted it in quantity.

Specification (SG510-4):
Calibre: 7·62mm NATO
Operation: Delayed blowback, selective fire
Length: 1016mm
Weight: 4·25kg
Barrel: 505mm, 4 grooves, right-hand twist
Magazine: 20-round box
Rate of fire: 500-650 rds/min.
Muzzle velocity: 790 m/sec.

The SG510 was the export model of the Swiss Army's Stgw57; it differs in the shape of the butt and is slightly lighter. The bipod seen here is more usually fitted to the sniping version which has mounting rails for a sighting telescope.

ASSAULT RIFLE SG550　　Switzerland

Manufacturer: SIG Swiss Industrial Company, Neuhausen-Rheinfalls Variant Model: SG551)

SIG continued development of rifles after the SG510 series, following it with the SG540 which was made under licence in France and sold widely throughout the world. Then, in the late 1970s, the Swiss Army asked for a design to fire the 5·56mm cartridge, and SIG produced the **SG550**. A competitive trial was held, the other entrant being a design from the Swiss Federal Arms Factory, and in 1983 the **SG550** was selected for adoption. Unfortunately, due to financial problems and the priority to provide some new tanks, the introduction of the new rifle was delayed until 1986, when it

went into service as the **StG.90**.

The **SG550** uses a conventional gas cylinder and piston driving a bolt carrier containing a rotating bolt. The hammer firing mechanism is capable of providing single shots, three-round bursts or automatic fire. The magazine is translucent so that the contents can be checked, and has studs on one side and sockets on the other so that two or three magazines can be clipped together. This allows any one magazine to be entered into the rifle, and when this is empty it is simply a matter of pulling the empty magazine free, shifting the set sideways and pushing the next magazine into place in order to continue firing.

Plastics are used for the butt and fore-

end, and the butt can be folded sideways to lie alongside the receiver. There is a light metal bipod which folds up beneath the fore-end when not required.

The standard sights are an aperture rear sight, fully adjustable for windage and elevation and a hooded blade foresight which can be height-adjusted for zeroing. The sights have luminous spots for aiming in poor light and these are part of the movable portion of the sight, so that adjustment of the day sight also adjusts the night sights. In addition, the top of the receiver is formed into a telescope mount to fit the standard Swiss Army optical and night vision sights; for export purposes, the NATO standard sight base can be

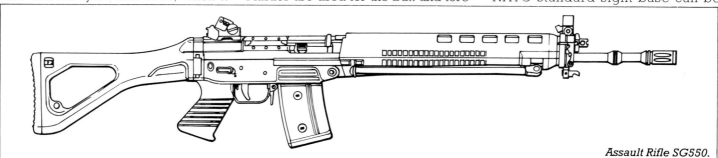

Assault Rifle SG550.

fitted if required.

The **SG551** is similar to the **SG550** but is a shorter carbine model using a 372mm barrel. The **SG550SP** and **551SP** are commercial versions of the **SG550** and **551**; they are only capable of single-shot fire and are designed so that they cannot be illegally converted back to automatic firing.

Top: SG550 standard rifle fitted with an experimental collimating (red dot) sight. Below: the standard-issue Stgw90 complete with cleaning kit, spare magazine and sling.

Specification (SG550):
Calibre: 5·56mm
Operation: Gas, selective fire
Length: 998mm butt extended; 772mm butt folded
Weight: 4·1kg with magazine & bipod
Barrel: 528mm, 6 grooves, right-hand twist
Magazine: 20- or 30-round box
Rate of fire: 700 rds/min.
Muzzle velocity: 995 m/sec.

ENFIELD SA80 (L85A1)

Manufacturer: Royal Small Arms Factory, Nottingham

Development of this rifle began in 1972 and it was first shown publicly in 1976. At that time it was built in 4·85mm calibre to suit a new cartridge developed specifically for this weapon. In 1977-80 the rifle and cartridge went through extensive NATO trials to determine the future NATO cartridge; the result was the adoption of the 5·56mm cartridge as standard, and the Enfield rifle therefore had to be redesigned in this calibre. This was not so hard as might be imagined, since the designers were alert to the possibility and had taken this into account in the initial design. A number of other modifications, resulting from experience gained in the trial, were incorporated into the design and it was finally introduced into British Army service in 1985.

The **L85A1** is a bullpup rifle, the action being set well back in the stock so as to give a compact overall length and yet have the maximum barrel length. The mechanism is a straight-forward gas piston operated rotating bolt in a bolt carrier, the carrier riding on rods inside the receiver. The standard infantry rifle is provided with the 'SUSAT' optical sight giving 4x magnification, with a small emergency open sight forming part of the optical sight casing. Non-infantry units are issued with a rifle having a carrying handle in place of the optical sight and with conventional iron sights.

Variant models include a Cadet rifle which fires only single shots and which can be converted to ·22 rimfire calibre; and a carbine version with short barrel. The **L85A1 rifle** is partnered by the **L86A1 Light Support Weapon**, a

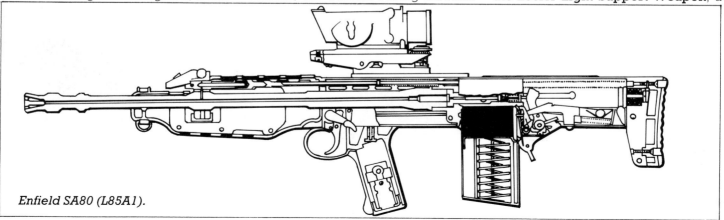

Enfield SA80 (L85A1).

heavy-barrelled version of the rifle for use as the squad light machine gun. Unfortunately the introduction of the Enfield system was followed by complaints from troops of defective weapons, magazines falling out, handguards falling off and sights which failed to keep their alignment. Much of this was exaggerated, and one has to expect some teething troubles in any new weapon, but there can be no doubt that quality control was negligent and far too many bad rifles reached the troops. In the course of closing down the Royal Small Arms Factory at Enfield and moving the rifle-making facility to the Royal Ordnance Factory Nottingham, the opportunity was taken to re-equip with entirely new machine tools and to tighten up quality control, and the quality of rifles produced since late 1988 is undoubtedly higher.

Specification:

Calibre: 5·56mm NATO
Operation: Gas, selective fire
Length: 785mm
Weight: 4·98kg with loaded magazine and sight
Barrel: 518mm, 6 grooves, right-hand twist
Magazine: 30-round box
Rate of fire: 940 m/sec.
Muzzle velocity: 845m/sec.

The British Army first essayed a bullpup rifle in the EM1 and EM2 of the late 1940s but were politically defeated by NATO. The L85 adopted the same principle but used a simpler mechanism. The infantry rifle is fitted with the SUSAT optical sight, while the remainder of the army used iron-sighted weapons.

RIFLE L96A1   UK

**Manufacturer: Accuracy
International Ltd, Portsmouth**

In the early 1980s the British Army began seeking a new sniping rifle; since the adoption of the FN-FAL as the service rifle, it had retained Lee-Enfield bolt-action rifles for sniping, but it was now time for a new weapon. Several models were extensively tested and the final selection was the **'Model PM Sniper'** made by Accuracy International, which was taken into service in 1986 as the **L96A1**.

The design is quite innovative; instead of the traditional wooden stock, the rifle is assembled to an aluminium frame which is then surrounded by a stock made of high-impact plastic material. This form of construction ensures that the rifle remains rigid even if the stock is struck or damaged, and so long as the frame is intact the rifle can still be used efficiently. Furthermore this form of construction does away with traditional methods of fixing and bedding barrels and actions into conventional stocks, making repair and maintenance much easier.

The stainless steel barrel is screwed into an extended receiver, which gives added support, and a locking ring, formed with lugs, is screwed tightly against the barrel. The three bolt lugs pass through this ring and, when the bolt is turned, lock behind the lugs; the bolt handle provides a fourth lug as it locks into the receiver. This locking ring simplifies manufacture and, when wear takes place and the cartridge

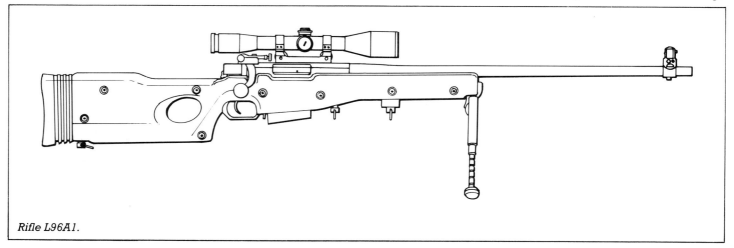

Rifle L96A1.

head clearance becomes excessive, a new ring can be fitted in a few minutes. Normal accuracy life of the barrel is well in excess of 5000 rounds.

The bolt operates in a 60° arc, two-thirds of the cocking action being performed during the opening stroke and the other third during the closing stroke, so evening out the bolt effort required. The firing pin travels only 6mm, ensuring a fast lock time.

The safety catch blocks the trigger, locks the bolt handle, and blocks the firing pin, totally preventing any accidental discharge even after violent blows.

There is a simple and robust telescope mount which allows the sight to be removed and replaced quickly without loss of zero. The standard telescope is either a Schmidt & Bender 10x42 or 2·5-10x56 zoom. Both are matched to a heavy match-grade bullet, and it is noticeable that the zoom telescope does not alter the point of impact as the zoom facility is used. Iron sights, capable of use to 700 metres range, are also fitted.

Specification:
Calibre: 7·62mm NATO
Operation: Manual, single-shot
Length: 1124-1194mm
Weight, empty: 6·50kg
Barrel: 655mm, 4 grooves, right-hand twist
Magazine: 10-round box
Muzzle velocity: 840 m/sec.

The L96A1 uses an aluminium 'chassis' to support the working parts, but clothes them in a plastic stock. The infantry version (left) has iron sights as standard; the special version below has no iron sights and a specially-designed flash hider.

BARRETT LIGHT FIFTY M82A1 — USA

Manufacturer: Barrett Firearms Mfg. Co., Murfreesboro, Tenn.

In the early 1980s the idea arose of using heavy precision rifles in order to snipe against material targets at long range; the scenario on view was that of a deep-intrusion raiding party setting up in cover some 1500 metres away from a forward airfield and then, with a quick series of well-aimed shots, putting all the aircraft out of action. After which they would simply abandon the weapon and make their escape. Many similar scenarios can be envisaged.

The **Barrett Light Fifty** is one of these rifles, and is a semi-automatic weapon firing the standard ·50 Browning heavy machine gun cartridge. The barrel and bolt carrier recoil after firing for about 25mm, after which the bolt is unlocked. The barrel stops moving and the bolt carrier and bolt are allowed to continue back, opening the bolt and extracting the spent case. A return spring is compressed during this movement, and the spring then drives the bolt forward to chamber a fresh round. The bolt locks and then the barrel and bolt assembly run forward

to the firing position.

The heavy barrel is fitted with a muzzle brake which, together with the recoil movement allowed to the barrel, absorbs a good deal of the recoil force and enables the gun to be fired from the shoulder in moderate comfort. The accuracy of the standard machine gun cartridge is marginal in this role, but the gradual acceptance of this type of rifle has seen the development of precision ammunition which gives good accuracy. In addition, there are a number of cartridges which have been developed for the Browning with

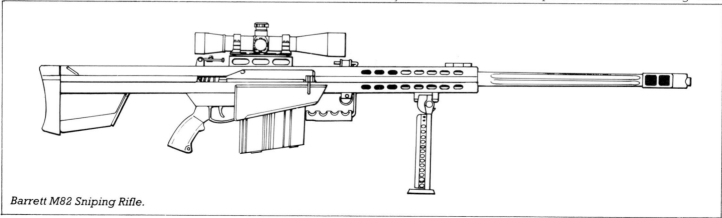

Barrett M82 Sniping Rifle.

considerable explosive and incendiary power, and using these will produce satisfactory results against the type of targets envisaged.

The **Light Fifty** is provided with an adjustable bipod, and it can also be fitted to most standard machine gun tripods. It is normally provided with a powerful telescope sight in order to allow use out to the maximum range of the ammunition, which can be up to 2000 metres, depending upon the type of target.

Specification:
Calibre: ·50 Browning
Operation: Short recoil, semi-automatic
Length: 1549mm
Weight: 14·7kg
Barrel: 838mm, 8 grooves, right-hand twist
Magazine: 11-round box
Muzzle velocity: 843 m/sec.

The Light Fifty uses the Browning .50 machine gun cartridge for long-range anti-materiel sniping. It is in use by US SEALs and by the British SAS.

RUGER MINI-14 RIFLE

USA

Manufacturer: Sturm, Ruger & Co, Southport, Conn.
(Variant Models: Ranch Rifle; Mini-Thirty; 14/20GB; AC-556; AC-556F)

This rifle was introduced in 1973 and was one of the first commercial semi-automatics in traditional form to fire the 5·56mm cartridge. The mechanism is very similar to that of the Garand, using an operating rod with a cam track to rotate and open the bolt, but the gas system is considerably different. The forward end of the operating rod ends in a cup-shaped piston which surrounds the gas cylinder, so that the rod is given sharp impulsive blows which gives it sufficient momentum to carry through the reloading cycle, but once the piston has moved away from the

gas port, the remaining gas is vented to the atmosphere. Thus the rod receives only as much impulse as it needs, and excessive recoil is avoided. As a result the **Mini-14** can be fired rapidly in relative comfort and without loss of control. Although initially offered commercially as a sporting weapon, the **Mini-14** is so compact and effective that it has been widely adopted by military and police forces in many countries.

A number of variant models followed the original design. The **'Ranch Rifle'** is simply a **Mini-14** with integral telescope mounting blocks; like the standard **Mini-14** it is available with a fixed wooden butt or a folding metal butt. The **Mini-Thirty** is the fixed-butt

version of the **Ranch Rifle** chambered and adjusted to fire the 7·62x39mm Soviet M43 cartridge. The **Mini-14/20GB** is a special adaptation of the standard **Mini-14** for military applications; there is a protected front sight which incorporates a bayonet mounting, a heat-resistant glass-fibre handguard, and a flash suppressor which also acts as a grenade launcher. The **AC-556** is similar to the **Mini-14/20GB** but has the additional capability of automatic fire. There is a selector lever on the right rear of the receiver which has three positions giving single shots, three-round bursts or automatic fire at approximately 750 rounds/minute. Finally the **AC-556F** is similar to the **AC-556** in providing

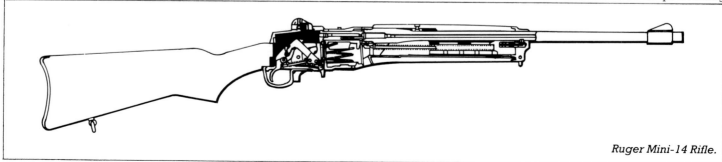

Ruger Mini-14 Rifle.

selective fire but has a much shorter barrel (330mm) and a folding metal strut butt and pistol grip. It is intended for use by crews of vehicles, airborne troops and others who have need of a more compact weapon than the standard **Mini-14**.

Resembling the M1 carbine, the Mini-14 was one of the first commercial semi-automatics to fire the 5.56mm cartridge, and it has become a popular weapon with police and security forces.

Specification:
Calibre: 5·56mm
Length: 946mm
Operation: Gas, semi-automtic
Weight: 2·90kg
Barrel: 470mm, 6 grooves, right-hand twist
Magazine: 5-, 10-, 20- or 30-round box
Rate of fire: 750 rds/min. (AC-556 and 556F)
Muzzle velocity: 1005 m/sec.

US RIFLE M16

Manufacturer: Colt's Patent Firearms Mfg Co., Hartford, Conn. (Variant Model: M16A1)

During and after the Korean War the US Operational Research Office undertook long studies of the effectiveness of rifle fire in combat; these led to Project Salvo, in which various ways of firing groups of small-calibre projectiles were explored. Out of Project Salvo came an Army request to the ArmaLite Division of the Fairchild Airplane and Engine Company to develop a ·22 calibre military rifle, since the Salvo trials and ORO studies

suggested that a small calibre would produce casualties as well as a larger calibre, and the small calibre meant less recoil and less weight for the soldier.

The result was the **ArmaLite AR-15** rifle, developed by Eugene Stoner; it ran into considerable opposition from the US Army, but eventually some 8500 were purchased by the US Air Force, and then, in 1963, it was adopted by the army as the **M16**. After experience in Vietnam the **M16A1** appeared in 1966; this adopted a positive bolt-closing device to force cartridges into

a fouled chamber.

The **M16** uses an unusual gas system of operation. Instead of the conventional gas piston, gas is tapped from the barrel and led back into the receiver by a tube which delivers the gas blast directly to the bolt carrier and thus blows it backwards. The bolt carrier has a cam track engaging a lug on the bolt, and as it moved, so it rotates and unlocks the bolt, then carries it back against the pressure of a return spring. At the same time a hammer mechanism is cocked. On the return stroke of the bolt a round is

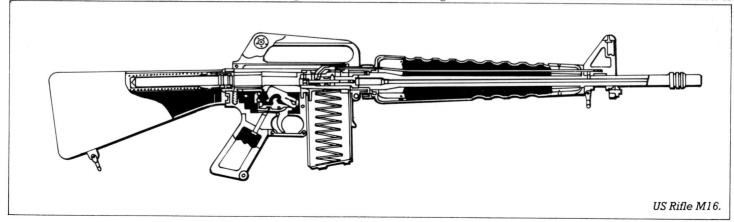

US Rifle M16.

driven from the magazine into the chamber, the bolt closes, and the remaining forward movement of the carrier rotates it to lock.

The system was designed around a particular type of propellant then in use by the US Army, but during the Vietnam war the specification for the propellant changed and this led to problems with the rifle. The bore and chamber were chromed, the bolt buffer changed to slow down the rate of automatic fire, and stricter instructions about cleaning were issued, which overcame the problem.

The **M16** (and **M16A1**) has been adopted by many other countries and has been manufactured under licence in Singapore, South Korea and the Philippine Republic. It is now being replaced in US service by the M16A2.

Specification:
Calibre: 5·56mm
Operation: Gas, selective fire
Length: 990mm
Weight: 2·86kg
Barrel: 508mm, 6 grooves, right-hand twist
Magazine: 30-round box
Rate of fire: 800 rds/min.
Muzzle velocity: 1000 m/sec.

The Colt/ArmaLite M16 is virtually the standard by which other assault rifles are compared. Capable of single shots or automatic fire it introduced the 5.56mm cartridge into military service.

US RIFLE M16A2

Manufacturer: Colt's Manufacturing Co. Inc., Hartford, Conn.

In 1977-80 the NATO countries carried out a long series of tests to settle on the cartridge which would replace the 7·62mm as the future NATO standard. The American 5·56mm, as used in the M16A1, was a hot favourite and eventually the 5·56mm cartridge was selected, but with a new bullet developed in Belgium known as the SS109. This was longer and heavier than the American M193 bullet and therefore it required a different twist of rifling in the barrel in order to perform properly. It followed that the US Army had either to re-barrel all its M16A1 rifles or find a new rifle suited to the new cartridge. Colt were approached with the problem, and they responded by producing an improved M16 with a heavier barrel. After some modification demanded by the Army, this was adopted in 1983 as the **M16A2** and has, by now, almost replaced the M16A1 in US service.

The **M16A2** differs from its predecessor in several respects. The barrel is heavier; but not entirely, since that part beneath the fore-end had to remain the same diameter as the M16A1 in order to fit the attachment of the M203 grenade launcher, but heavy enough to be stiffer and therefore more accurate than that of the M16A1.

Instead of the full-automatic option of the M16A1, the new rifle has a three-round burst mechanism, a device permitting three shots to be fired for one trigger pressure. Since most experienced troops fire short bursts in automatic fire, this merely mechanises the task and also prevents the rifle climbing out of control in an over-long burst. The barrel is, of course, rifled at one turn in 7 inches so as to suit the new standard bullet, and the rear sight has been improved. A new flash suppressor on the muzzle omits the bottom slot of the earlier rifle, so preventing dust being blown into the air in prone firing and also eliminating a rush of gas downwards which tended

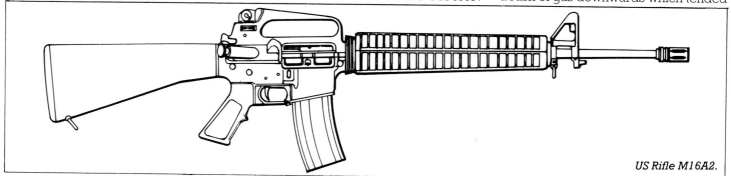

US Rifle M16A2.

to thrust the muzzle up. There is also a cartridge case deflector on the side of the receiver which directs the ejected case away from the face of a left-handed firer.

The **M16A2** has also been adopted by the Canadian Army as the **C7** rifle; in their case, the full-automatic option has been chosen instead of the three-round burst. There is also an **M16A2 Carbine**, with a shorter barrel and a collapsible butt; this is used by the Canadian Army as their **C8 Carbine**.

Specification:
Calibre: 5·56mm NATO
Operation: Gas, selective fire
Length: 1006mm
Weight: 3·58kg
Barrel: 508mm, 6 grooves, right-hand twist
Magazine: 30-round box
Rate of fire: 600-940 rds/min.
Muzzle velocity: 991 m/sec.

The M16A2 has a heavier barrel, better sights, a cooler handguard and a three-round burst feature. It is seen here, below, with a Magnavox infra-red night sight fitted.

US CARBINE M1

**Manufacturer: Winchester
Repeating Arms Co and others
(Variant Models: M1A1, M2, M3)**

In 1938 the US Army requested a light rifle for arming second-line troops and weapon crews who did not require a full-power rifle. The idea was turned down, but resubmitted in 1940 and manufacturers approached. A suitable cartridge was developed, and 11 competing designs were tested in May 1941. As it happened, the Winchester company had a light rifle in the course of development as a private venture and this, modified to meet the military specification, was accepted as the **Carbine M1** in September 1941.

The carbine uses a very similar bolt action to the Garand rifle, but the gas action is very different and was the first military application of what is now called a 'tappet' or 'short-stroke piston'. There is a short gas cylinder beneath the barrel which contains a captive piston. An operating rod, connected to the bolt by the same sort of curved plate and cam track as the Garand, lies in contact with the piston. On firing, gas is vented into the cylinder and drives the light piston back very sharply, giving the operating rod an impulsive blow which is sufficient to drive it back and open the bolt. A return spring around the rod

then pulls the bolt back to load the next round from a conventional box magazine. There is a hammer mechanism similar to that of the Garand to fire the cartridge.

As a short-range self-defence weapon the carbine was satisfactory, but the bullet is no more than a pistol bullet and at ranges over about 150 yards it is neither accurate nor very effective. Nevertheless, it was light and handy and became a popular weapon, several million being made by numerous contractors.

Soon after its introduction the **M1A1** appeared; this had a folding metal butt and the weapon was intended for

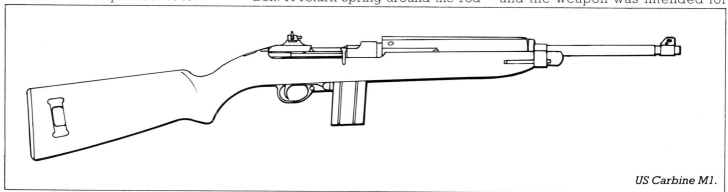

US Carbine M1.

airborne and other troops who required a more compact weapon. Then came a demand for automatic fire, and the **M2** was introduced; this was precisely the same as the **M1** but with the addition of a switch on the firing mechanism which allowed automatic fire. With this came a curved 30-round magazine to supplement the original 15-round magazine. Finally, the **M3** was a special version of the **M2** with fittings to take an infra-red night sight developed in 1944.

Specification:
Calibre: ·30 Carbine M1
Operation (M1): Gas, semi-automatic
Length: 905mm
Weight: 2·48kg
Barrel: 457mm, 4 grooves, right-hand twist
Magazine: 15- or 30-round box
Rate of fire: 750 rds/min. (M2 and M3 only)
Muzzle velocity: 593 m/sec.

The M1 Carbine was everybody's light and handy favourite weapon, and over six million were made between 1941 and 1945. Since then several commercial companies have made thousand of copies.

Glossary

Blowback

A type of automatic pistol in which the breech block or bolt is not positively locked to the barrel at the moment of firing. When fired, the explosion pressure inside the cartridge case drives it back and thus opens the breech. Safety is achieved by having the mass of the breech sufficient to resist the movement for the split second it takes the bullet to go up the barrel and leave the muzzle, after which the breech pressure drops; but by that time the breech has been given sufficient momentum for it to open.

Box Magazine

A form of ammunition supply where the cartridges are contained in a metal box, either detachable from the weapon or forming part of it, and are propelled towards the mouth of the magazine by a spring so as to enter the feedway of the weapon.

Calibre

The diameter of the weapon's barrel, measured internally from land to land, the land being that part of the barrel which lies between the rifling grooves. Alternatively, the diameter of a cylinder which will just pass through the barrel.

Caseless Cartridge

A cartridge which does not use the ordinary brass or other metal case to contain the propellant and carry the bullet and cap. It consists, instead, of a solid block of special propellant in which the bullet and cap are embedded; additionally, the cap is also of some combustible material. The result is that after firing there is no empty case or residue to be extracted, and thus reloading can take place much more quickly. It demands a very well sealed breech, since in an ordinary weapon the cartridge case expands to firm the seal.

Centre Fire

A cartridge in which the primer cap is placed centrally in the base.

Chamber

Enlarged and specially shaped portion of the barrel into which the cartridge is loaded in order to fire.

Cylinder

Component of a revolver in which the chambers are bored. This is held behind the barrel on an axis or arbor so that it can be revolved by some mechanism, usually connected to the trigger, so as to position each cylinder in turn behind the barrel.

Delayed Blowback

An automatic weapon in which the bolt is not positively locked to the barrel at the instant of firing but in which the rearward blowback movement of the bolt is slowed down by some mechanism so that there is resistance to opening until the bullet is well clear of the barrel.

Disconnector

Part of the firing mechanism of a self-loading weapon which disconnects the trigger after each shot and does not re-connect it until the firer releases the trigger. It prevents the weapon firing in automatic mode.

Double Action

A firing mechanism which permits two modes of operation. The hammer can be manually cocked and then released by pressing the trigger (single action); or the hammer can be cocked and released by a single continuous pressure on the trigger. Common in revolvers, less common in automatic pistols.

Gas Operation

A method of operating an automatic or self-cocking weapon. In the most common form, some of the gas driving the bullet is allowed to pass through a hole in the barrel and strike a piston-head; this is driven back and, in turn, forces back an operating arm which opens the breech and, at the same time, compresses a spring. The gas pressure is then allowed to escape and the spring expands, forcing the arm back to re-load and close the breech ready for the next shot.

Magazine Safety

A safety device in automatic pistols which prevents firing once the magazine has been removed. It prevents the common accident when a round is left in the chamber and later fired by someone who thought the gun was empty.

Receiver

The 'body' of a firearm, to which the barrel, stock, grip, sights and so on are attached, and inside which is the bolt or breech and firing mechanism.

Recoil Operation

Method of operation for a self-loading or automatic weapon which relies upon the recoil of the barrel after firing. May be 'long' or 'short' recoil; in the former, the barrel and closed breech move back a distance longer than the length of a complete cartridge, after which the breech is opened and held, while the barrel runs forward again. The breech is then released to load the weapon. In short recoil weapons the barrel and closed breech move back slightly, after which the breech is unlocked and the barrel stops, leaving the breech free to move back to complete the loading cycle.

Velocity

The speed of the bullet; generally given either in metres per second or feet per second. Defined as 'Muzzle Velocity' when referring to the speed as the bullet leaves the weapon; 'Observed Velocity', the speed at any particular point during its flight; and 'Remaining Velocity', the speed at the end of its flight.

Windage

Term used in two senses:- 1) the clearance between a muzzle-loaded bullet and the barrel, which allows the bullet to be loaded, or 2) an allowance given in taking aim so as to compensate for the effect of wind upon the bullet's flight. This can be done by moving the rear sight to one side or the other, and such movement is called 'windage'.

Zero

A weapon is 'zeroed' when the sights are adjusted so that the bullet will strike the point of aim at some specified distance. From this 'zero point' the sight adjustment mechanism will be able to alter the sight line for different ranges so that the bullet strike still coincides with the point of aim. But unless the zeroing is done by the person who intends to use the weapon, with the ammunition he intends to use, full benefit cannot be obtained, since the act of zeroing takes into account personal eyesight, the way he holds the weapon and other intangibles.